ASSESSMENT
in
PERSPECTIVE
Focusing on the Reader Behind the Numbers

Clare Landrigan & Tammy Mulligan
Foreword by Gail Boushey and Joan Moser, "The Sisters"

Stenhouse Publishers
Portland, Maine

Stenhouse Publishers
www.stenhouse.com

Credits

Figure 2.1: From *Reading with Meaning* by Debbie Miller, copyright © 2002, reproduced with permission of Stenhouse Publishers. www.stenhouse.com

Figure 5.7: From *The CAFE Book: Engaging All Students in Daily Literacy Assessment & Instruction* by Gail Boushey and Joan Moser ("The Sisters"), copyright © 2009, reproduced with permission of Stenhouse Publishers. www.stenhouse.com

Figure S5.3: Reprinted with permission from *Benchmark Assessment System I, Second Edition, Assessment Forms* by Irene C. Fountas and Gay Su Pinnell. Copyright © 2011, 2008 by Irene C. Fountas and Gay Su Pinnell. Published by Heinemann, Portsmouth, NH. All rights reserved.

Figure 6.1: From *Opening Minds* by Peter Johnston, copyright © 2012, reproduced with permission of Stenhouse Publishers. www.stenhouse.com

Library of Congress Cataloging-in-Publication Data
Landrigan, Clare.
    Assessment in perspective : focusing on the reader behind the numbers / Clare
Landrigan and Tammy Mulligan ; foreword by Gail Boushey and Joan Moser, "The Sisters".
    pages cm
    Includes bibliographical references and index.
    ISBN 978-1-57110-964-4 (pbk. : alk. paper)—ISBN 978-1-57110-989-7 (e-book) 1.
Educational tests and measurements—United States. 2. Academic achievement—United
States. 3. Educational evaluation—United States. I. Title.
    LB3051.L287 2013
    371.26—dc23
                                                                                2012050483

Cover design, interior design, and typesetting by Martha Drury
Photographs courtesy of Gelfand-Piper Photography

Manufactured in the United States of America

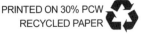
PRINTED ON 30% PCW
RECYCLED PAPER

19 18 17 16 15 14 13   9 8 7 6 5 4 3 2 1

Dedicated to

Our husbands, Chris and George, for keeping us laughing and supporting our new ideas, ventures, and aspirations.

Abby, Jack, Connor, and Ryan, for bringing joy into our lives, reminding us what is most important and inspiring us every day.

All the educators who open their classroom doors and share their knowledge, wisdom, and questions with us so we can continue to learn and grow.

Contents

Foreword by Gail Boushey and Joan Moser, "The Sisters"   *vii*

Preface   *ix*

Acknowledgments   *xi*

Chapter 1:   **Moving Beyond the Numbers:**
Finding the Stories of Our Readers   **1**

Chapter 2:   **Why Assessment? Why Now?**   **7**

Chapter 3:   **Assessment Literacy**   **19**

Chapter 4:   **Triangulating Assessment**   **45**

Chapter 5:   **Assessing Authentically, Every Day**   **71**

Chapter 6:   **The Student's Role in Assessment**   **99**

Epilogue   **123**

Appendix   *125*

Bibliography   *131*

Index   *135*

Foreword

By Gail Boushey and Joan Moser,
"The Sisters"

Whether you are a teacher, a principal, an instructional assistant, a coach, or an assessment coordinator, this book should be added to your "must read" list, especially if you've ever felt a disconnect between mandatory assessments and your day-to-day work with students.

We have been fans of Clare and Tammy's work since we first met them. Our initial interactions with these two dynamic teachers and staff developers left us inspired by their perpetual positive language as they conversed about the amazing teachers and children with whom they work. Over time Tammy and Clare's affirmative attitudes also influenced our thinking about assessments, even those assessments mandated by schools. They helped us realize that all assessment can play a role in understanding the story of each and every child. These two passionate teachers so eloquently speak—and now write—about the power of a correctly matched assessment when working with students and how a strong assessment should not be thought of as merely taking away from instructional time.

Clare and Tammy write, "Assessments should not be about defining a reader but about piecing together information to help us design classroom experiences so we can observe our readers learning and understand what each one needs." We've always believed, just as Tammy and Clare do, that our children are more than an assessment score, that assessment and instruction are inseparable, and that instruction can meet high standards and still be developmentally appropriate. We understand the importance of finding the best assessments to discern our students' needs. In our second book, *The CAFE Book: Engaging All Students in Daily Literacy Assessment and Instruction*, we write about using assessments as a guide to match students to their next most-needed reading strategy on our CAFE Menu for just-in-time learning. The power of Tammy and Clare's book is that it helps answer the question of which assessment will best guide us so we know what to teach next!

What also makes this book unique is the way that Tammy and Clare have set out to help us understand assessment tools. Knowing that all assessments are designed differently, and are for different purposes, they examine a wide range of assessments, listing the strengths and limitations of each and providing examples and purposes of assessments that are currently popular as well as ones that should be used more generally. *Assessment in Perspective* is a brilliant and clear reference that will enhance the assessment literacy of all educators.

Clare and Tammy teach us how to view mandated common assessments as just one piece of information that, when triangulated with other data, will inform and guide our teaching. They share the importance of not being satisfied with a single data point for a child but instead gathering formal and informal data to gain a whole picture of that child. When that whole picture is in place, we are able to provide the requisite and timely instruction that will move the child forward. By becoming more knowledgeable about the available assessments, we are better able to determine which assessments will help us assemble that picture.

We believe this book is a must-have for all educators. It is the perfect guide to maximizing the benefit of assessments; it will help us to truly know, understand, and teach all of our children. Clare and Tammy are top-notch teachers and world-class human beings. In this age of assessment, they are just what we need to keep assessment in perspective.

Preface

Words mean more than what is set down on paper. It takes the human voice to infuse them with deeper meaning.

—Maya Angelou

We have been working together since 1994. We have cotaught in classrooms, codirected a district curriculum leader position, coached together, and are now staff developers together. Our current role as staff developers—or, as we like to think of it, collaborators in teaching—allows us to learn with hundreds of teachers in schools that represent a wide range of socioeconomic and demographic factors. It is a privilege to teach with teachers, observe their brilliance, and learn collaboratively every day. The dialogue we have with these educators brings clarity to our thinking and continually inspires new questions for us.

When we began writing this book, we struggled with how to structure it so that we could share all that we learn in these classrooms and have it reflect the many voices we learn from each day. One late night in the midst of writing, we looked at each other and asked, "How can we bring this dynamic nature of assessment to life on the written page?" Neither of us answered. We just ordered another cup of tea and sat in silence. Then it came to us . . . the conversations, the dialogue, and the stories. We will bring the teachers, the readers, and the classroom moments we have learned from into this book by sharing these stories.

In this book the voice of "we" represents our—Tammy and Clare's—perspective on what we have learned about assessment.

Although we are continually learning with others, this book is a reflection of our thinking, our learning, and our journey in understanding assessment and instruction.

Acknowledgments

It is good to have an end to journey toward; but it is the journey that matters in the end.

—Ernest Hemingway

Through the years we have met and worked with many people who have inspired, taught, and mentored us. We could never begin to acknowledge each person who has been a part of our journey, but it is clear to us how each step has directly influenced who we are and what we believe as educators.

We'd like to thank our colleagues at the Eliot-Pearson Children's School: Janet Stork, who always believed in us; Betty Nolden Allen, who always pushed our thinking; Debbie LeeKeenan, who taught us the importance of believing in each learner; and Sue Steinseck and Stephanie Curtis, who helped us bring our ideas to life.

At the Center for Applied Child Development at Tufts University, we are grateful for Lynn Schade's passion for professional development, Marcia Uretsky's knowledge of literacy and leadership, and Martha Heller-Winokur's gift for listening to students.

Thanks to the following people at Wayland Public Schools in Massachusetts: Gary Burton for taking a chance on us; Wayne Ogden for being a "one of a kind" mentor; Brad Crozier, Sue Abrams, and Cyndy Dunham for teaching us about shared leadership; the Lab Room Classroom Teachers for teaching us the true meaning of collaboration; and all the teachers in Wayland for learning with us every day.

And then there are our friends at Choice Literacy:

Brenda Power helped us find our voice and was the first to recognize that our work was really about assessment.

Franki Sibberson constantly encouraged us to share our thinking and was the first to say, "Girls, you need to write a book."

Jennifer Allen convinced us that this topic was important and gave us the push we needed.

Gail Boushey and Joan Moser inspired us to do what we believe and to love what we do.

We deeply appreciate the teachers, administrators, and coaches we work with every day (you all know who you are) for your support, help, flexibility, and patience. You gave us the courage to do this. Our friends and neighbors who cooked dinners, drove carpools, and listened to us—we could not have pulled it off without you. Thanks to Chris Landrigan, Chris Augusta-Scott, Jason DiCarlo, and Cathy Milton for their endless conversation, reading of drafts, feedback, and words of encouragement.

Thank you to the Stenhouse crew—Chris Downey, Jay Kilburn, Martha Drury, Rebecca Eaton, and Jill Cooley—for guiding us through our first publication and bringing our book to life.

Thank you, Philippa Stratton and Jennifer Allen, for understanding what we were trying to say long before we did and for helping us put it into writing. You listened when we needed to talk and guided when we needed it most. We can never put into words how grateful we are to the both of you.

And finally, we thank our families. You have seen us through every step of this journey. You have always loved our stories from the classroom, and you helped us see the importance in them. We could never have done this without you, and we love you more than words can say. And yes, the book is finished!

CHAPTER 1

Moving Beyond the Numbers

Finding the Stories of Our Readers

---

*Their story, yours and mine—it's all we carry with us on this trip we take and
we owe it to each other to respect our stories and learn from them.*

—William Carlos Williams

▶ Madeline was a student in our class for two years. She had significant special needs. Madeline came to us with more quantitative data than we thought could exist on one person. There was file after file after file. We spent weeks reading about her before we even met her. We began planning and creating materials before school began. We had it covered—we were all set. Then we met Madeline. Not only could we not use the beautiful materials we made, but we could not even get her off the top of the playground structure to come into the classroom. Educators who wanted to learn about inclusion observed us—they wanted to see "how it was done." Can you see it? Twenty educators with clipboards, taking notes as we are trying to coax her off the top of the monkey bars. Not pretty. We read the files, we analyzed the assessments, we did the planning, we were ready. Why was this not working? Our mentor at the time, Betty Noldon Allen, sat down with us one afternoon and after listening to us talk for about thirty minutes, simply said, "So, who *is* Madeline? Get to know Madeline. Teach her and notice how she learns, what engages her, and what she needs to learn. If you don't understand her as a learner in your classroom, then you will never be able to teach her." ◀

Assessment is more than a published test or tool that is administered formally. Assessment is also the data we collect authentically, every day. It is humbling to look back at how we approached assessment with Madeline. We meant well, but we rushed to find the answers to how to teach her by looking only at the formal data given to us rather than combining that information with our observations of her in our classroom.

Lucy Calkins talks about the "act of assessing" when she describes assessment practices in *The Nuts and Bolts of Teaching Writing* (2003). She says, "Assessment is the thinking teacher's mind work. The intelligence that guides our every moment as a teacher" (85). It is through this "mind work"—collecting data, asking questions, digging deeper, talking with colleagues, and putting the pieces of information together—that we can truly understand our readers and find their stories.

Calkins's definition of assessment rings true, but since 2002, when the high-stakes testing climate began, it has been difficult to keep this definition alive. The No Child Left Behind Act has caused those in our profession to focus more on administering assessments, reporting quantitative data, and accountability and less on understanding the assessments we are using and the type of information they can provide about our readers. Many of us have been so busy trying to implement an assessment plan that little time is left to use it to understand our students. What's worse is that the value being placed on "high-stakes" tests has caused teachers to question how the classroom assessments we have always used to guide our instruction fit into the equation.

There have been days—okay, maybe months—when these changes in our profession leave us feeling like we are drowning in data. Yet we know that buried within all these data are the stories of our students as readers. We cannot afford to lose these stories. We are pushing ourselves to remember that behind every number is a reader and that we, as teachers, have the power to use assessment to make a difference for each one of them.

We know everyone has a humbling teacher moment like our "Madeline story"—personally, we have quite a few. Teaching is never perfect. "There is no such thing as the perfect lesson, the perfect day in school, or the perfect teacher. For teachers and students alike, the goal is not perfection but the persistence in the pursuit of understanding important things" (Tomlinson and McTighe 2006, 56). There is also no such thing as the perfect assessment or assessment plan. We think we can all agree that assessment as it stands today in our profession as elementary educators is far from perfect. Assessment to us, however, is not only about a tool and the information it provides; it is about what we do with that tool and information. Assessment is about the pursuit of understanding our readers, and what we do in that act makes a difference in the life of a reader. When we reflect on our teaching journey, from Madeline to now, we realize that the greatest learning has always come from the conversations we have about readers with our colleagues.

Assessment is a controversial topic (and some say a dry topic) to be writing about, but many of you and your stories have inspired us to advocate for the true role of assessment in our profession. In this book we share the stories of the many educators who open their classroom doors and share their knowledge, wisdom, and questions with us so we can continue to learn. We hope that through sharing stories of real classrooms, we will bring the dynamic nature of assessment to life in a way that will engage you in a dialogue as you read. These stories are not about perfection, but about the pursuit of moving beyond the numbers to find the stories of our readers. There is a medical truism that says, "Eighty percent of the time, a diagnosis can be made on history—the diagnosis is often in the story." We find that the greatest potential in assessment is also in the story. We hope you agree.

THE STORIES WE CARRY

What Constitutes Data?

Suzanne is a mentor teacher. Her classroom is a place of rigor, inquiry, and joy. During one of our grade-level coaching sessions, she just did not seem herself. After the session, I approached her.

"Is everything okay? You did not seem yourself today."

"I don't know. I just think this is all a waste of time. I know my kids. I don't need these data. Teaching has become about testing, and that is not why I went into this job." The silence sat for a few minutes. "Do you think I am negative?" she asked.

"No, not at all. I am just wondering how you know your kids. Isn't that data?"

"Well, no. Those are just my notes and observations. I am talking about the data."

"I guess I see those both as data. I think both give me information I need to either confirm my thoughts about a reader or help me understand that reader's needs."

"I guess I never thought of it that way. I am just so sick of the testing."

"Well, there we agree. But if we don't use the results, isn't it an even bigger waste of time? What if we start our next session with your classroom notes and find some questions we have about some of your readers? Then we can take a look at the formal data to see if they give us any insights."

Suzanne, the lifelong learner, smiled and said, "I still hate the testing, but let's give it a try next week."

Using Observations to Dig Deeper

Nate came to first grade excited to learn. He loved stories, art, and music. He began first grade knowing all his letters, and in kindergarten he had been reading Level C books. During independent reading he always appeared engaged, but during partner reading, he always needed to get a drink or go to the bathroom when it was his turn to read. We spoke to him about this, but it continued. We also began to notice a difference during writing workshop when we encouraged him to add words to his incredible illustrations. We decided to just observe Nate and take notes throughout the day and see what we noticed. Our notes clearly showed us that Nate was not as engaged as we had thought and in fact was a master of getting answers from other people before he raised his hand in large-group settings or shared his thoughts when in small groups. We then began to really observe him reading text that was unfamiliar to him. He could not do it. We had him read familiar text and noticed that he did not have one-to-one correspondence. It appeared that he memorized the text and repeated it verbatim. His eyes barely skimmed the text. Nate began intervention sessions four times a week, but he still did not progress. He was motivated, but nothing seemed to click. One day, we had an artist visit our classroom. During our morning meeting the kids were buzzing about the upcoming visit. Nate was clearly agitated.

"What's wrong, Nate? Is everything okay?"

"NO!" he shouted. "I love art. Why didn't anyone tell me an artist is coming? Why did you tell everyone but me?"

"They didn't *tell* us, Nate," his friend Robert cautiously shared. "It's written on the schedule—right there," he said, pointing.

Nate looked at us confused. Then he got up, walked to the schedule, and said, "Where is it?"

We pointed to the words on the schedule and said, "It's right here with all the things we write about our schedule each morning."

Nate paused, took a deep breath, and said, "So you mean you write what we are going to do each day up on the board and all the kids read it and that is how everyone knows what is going to happen each morning?"

"Yes, Nate."

"Well, that makes so much sense. I was wondering how everyone else always knew what was happening and I never knew."

That was the moment Nate understood the concepts of print. The morning schedule turned out to be our most powerful piece of assessment. Nate ended the year on bench-mark.

CHAPTER 2

Why Assessment? Why Now?

What if you have district mandates that run counter to your beliefs? Take the high road. Don't let them defeat you. Do what you have to do; in the end no one can mandate how you feel about children, the ways you interact with them throughout the day, and the things you say and do that reflect who you are and what you believe about teaching and learning.

—Debbie Miller, *Teaching with Intention* (2008)

▶ We were going to see Debbie Miller! We arrived early, secured seats up front and center, and were ready with pen in hand to take notes on every word she said about teaching comprehension to young readers. We were very surprised by how she began the session. She held up a book, *Two or Three Things I Know for Sure* by Dorothy Allison (1995), and talked to us about an experience she had with a professor named Brian Cambourne. He encouraged Debbie to make explicit her beliefs about teaching and learning and to know the theory behind her beliefs. She then had each of us stop and reflect on the two or three things we "know for sure" about teaching and learning. Debbie showed us her beliefs and where she hung them in her classroom so that she could constantly hold true to the research that guides her while she continues to learn and try new practices. This made us really think about change in our profession. How do we stay open to new research and theories on best practice while staying grounded in what we believe to be true about children and teaching? How can we be lifelong learners and still have guiding principles? We came home and shared this experience with colleagues in our district. We realized how important it is to have this conversation with our colleagues and talk with each other about the reasons behind our decisions and our thoughts. When we share the why behind our thinking, we understand each other's guiding principles and can leave ourselves open to learn from one another. ◀

When we thought through the two or three things we know for sure, we realized that it was difficult for us to separate our beliefs from the research we hold dear. We found ourselves listing researchers and theories rather than beliefs. We pushed ourselves to try to link these researchers to two or three big beliefs that we know for sure and noticed that assessment was central to many of our beliefs. This was surprising to us at first. Assessment was not something either of us thought of as our passion or focus. The more we reflected, however, the more we realized that most of what we believe really is about assessment or understanding our readers. This is how it turned out.

Two or Three Things We Know for Sure

1. Assessment is more than a number.

Assessment needs to be the vehicle that moves us beyond defining our readers as a number. Assessment should not be about defining a reader but about piecing together information to help us design classroom experiences so we can observe our readers learning and understand what each one needs.

The research that guides this belief:

Marie Clay was the researcher and teacher who introduced us to the idea of systematic observation. She presented observation surveys that were reliable enough to compare one child with another and one child on two different occasions, but that also reflected the work a child actually did in the classroom as a reader. She provided systematic ways to obtain information through observation so teachers could find the patterns they needed to understand why students were doing what they were doing and subsequently design instruction to meet their needs.

Peter Johnston is the professor who taught us to pay attention to the language we use as we teach readers in our classrooms. He taught us to think carefully about what we say to young learners and how our words can empower readers. Johnston's research on the power of a teacher's words pushed us to think about how we collect formative assessment data in the classroom. When we talk with students and document our conversations, we gather information about what our readers are thinking, what they believe are important next steps in their learning process, and how they perceive their role in the task of reading.

2. Assessment and instruction are inseparable.

Purposeful instruction is based on assessment. Assessment allows us to differentiate our teaching to meet our readers' needs. When we instruct, we watch how readers respond and use these data to adjust our instruction.

The research that guides this belief:

Carol Ann Tomlinson is the educator who first pushed us to think about the range of learners in our classroom, shift our thinking around assessment, and differentiate our instruction. She pushed us to remember that assessment is not about what happened but about what is going to happen next: "Assessment is today's means to modify tomorrow's instruction" (1999, 10). She changed the way we thought about using assessment to help us think about and revise our instruction in specific ways for individual or small groups of students.

Pearson and Gallagher are the researchers who developed the gradual release of responsibility model of instruction (1983). The model gives us several opportunities for collecting assessment data during instruction. This framework for teaching includes teachers coaching students as they learn a new strategy and observing how students apply new learning. When students are working collaboratively and independently, we listen in on their conversations and observe how they use a new reading strategy. We take systematic notes to give us insights about what the students understand and what is confusing to them. This model allows us to take a step back, watch our students in action, and collect authentic assessment data during instruction. (See Figure 2.1.)

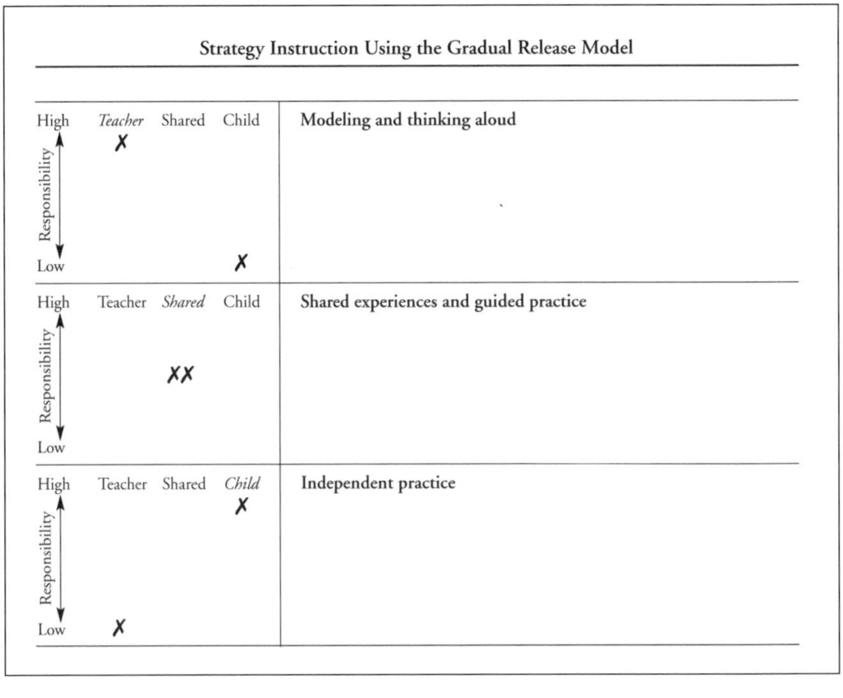

Figure 2.1
This model by Debbie Miller shows a student's level of responsibility during each phase of learning. Each level provides an opportunity to collect assessment data. The higher the level of responsibility a student has, the more opportunity we have to observe and assess his or her understanding.

Strategy Instruction Using the Gradual Release Model

	Teacher	Shared	Child	**Modeling and thinking aloud**
High	X			
Responsibility				
Low			X	

	Teacher	*Shared*	Child	**Shared experiences and guided practice**
High				
Responsibility		XX		
Low				

	Teacher	Shared	*Child*	**Independent practice**
High			X	
Responsibility				
Low	X			

3. Our instruction can meet high standards and still be developmentally appropriate.

The developmental theory of learning guides our beliefs and our understanding of how children learn. No matter what standards or curriculum we are asked to teach, we always think about how to create a developmental approach to teaching those high standards.

The research that guides this belief:

Jean Piaget was the first psychologist to complete a systematic study of cognitive development. He introduced us to the idea that children are not simply "miniature adults" but actually think in very different ways. Through his research, we learned that there are particular stages in child development (sensorimotor, preoperational, concrete operational, formal operational) and that each one is categorized by specific observable behaviors. It is through observing, asking questions, and watching children as they work with concrete materials that we can understand a particular learner's stage of development.

Piaget also taught us that learners not only progress through these stages as they grow and mature, but that they grow through experiencing things in their environment. As children experience discrepancies between what they already know and what they discover, they learn new ideas and concepts. Piaget labeled these learning processes assimilation, accommodation, and equilibrium. This research helped us understand that children need learning experiences that build on what they know and challenge their current understandings. Learning experiences that push learners to analyze their own misconceptions and construct knowledge help children learn and grow.

Lev Vygotsky introduced us to the zone of proximal development—the difference between what a learner can do without help and what he or she can do with help. This affected how we observed our students and redefined our understanding of using assessment. Assessment was no longer only about what students can do well, but also what students do when they are faced with problems. He introduced us to the importance of watching to see what skills and strategies students use when faced with a challenge and then using those observations to understand what they know well and to inform our next steps in instruction.

***

Although these are the things we believe and know for sure, we are still lifelong learners. As we continue to learn professionally, we always think about new ideas by questioning them in relation to our understanding of these beliefs. Everything we learn needs to make sense to us in terms of what we know about kids and how they learn new concepts. Piaget's theory of learning through assimilation and accommodation explains how we can stick to what we know to be true and yet learn new information that challenges our current understandings. New research pushes us to analyze not only what we think is important, but why we think it is important as we construct new knowledge and incorporate it into our practice.

We think it is more important now than it has ever been for us to balance knowing our beliefs with being open to learning about new methods in assessment and the practice of teaching reading. Our world is ever changing, and there is a constant stream of new information about the practice of teaching for us to process. As educators our job has always been to prepare our students for the workforce. Today, however, we have absolutely no idea what kind of workforce we are preparing our kindergarten students for; technology has made it a moving target. The digital world has affected and will continue to affect our readers. Research is helping us understand what our students need to learn to be effective readers in the twenty-first century, but we need to remember that the students sitting in front of us still learn as they always have developmentally. If only human development worked like the Apple Store and a "new generation iKid" was developed each year to keep up with the changing technological demands of our world. The digital world may be pushing us to a place that none of us can even imagine, but the way readers develop as human learners is a constant. (See Figure 2.2.)

Many aspects of our world have shifted to the abstract realm. Even things like baseball, drawing, and Legos can now be done virtually. Our pedagogy taught us the importance of young learners constructing their knowledge and testing their understanding. Elementary educators know how important it is for our learners to test, retest, and test again to progress through cognitive dissonance to understanding. Kids are not developmentally different from how they were at the beginning of our career in this profession, but what we are asking of kids is very different. The question for us is how to prepare our students to live in the twenty-first century while still teaching in a way that is developmentally appropriate. For us, assessment is the answer to that question.

Assessment is a window into understanding how our readers are approaching a text and what is confusing to them. It is through

Figure 2.2
Our young readers continually remind us how confusing this new world is to a concrete, developmental learner by the comments they make and the observations they share with us in the classroom.

> "Why do we need a job? We can just get one of those cards that you put in a wall. You know, you put it in the wall and money comes out."
>
> "Why do I need to learn to read? I will just get one of those Kindle things and it will read to me. Isn't that reading?"
>
> "Let's just Google it. It's faster and you don't have to read as much."
>
> "What do you mean, put it in an envelope? Can't we just hit 'send'?"
>
> "Why do I have to learn to make a movie in my mind when I can just go see a movie?"
>
> "Reading is boring. I like how fast everything is on a TV or a computer. A book is just there—it doesn't do anything."

observing their actions and noting their responses that we understand how we need to teach them. It is through the act of assessing that we create learning experiences in our classrooms that reflect how our students learn. We observe them in the moment they are experiencing cognitive dissonance and note how they respond to our scaffolding. When we create learning experiences that push our students to think, problem-solve, and synthesize, we are creating an environment of authentic assessment. There is no better way to understand readers than to watch as they construct meaning from text. Only teachers— not published tools and not tests—know our readers well enough to design learning experiences that can inform us and scaffold their learning.

Thinking about assessment in this way is hard to do in a time when so much focus is on accountability and standards. The shift to data-based reform "has had less happy consequences. In many schools, it has morphed into an unintended obstacle to both effective instruction and intellectually rich, forward-looking education" (Schmoker 2008/2009, 70). We find it important to remember our beliefs about the true role of formative assessment in our daily teaching. This is not to say that we do not find formal assessments useful—we do. They are useful if we use them as one piece of the story. When we take all the information we have from the classroom and the formal assessments and tests, we have a balance of assessment types to gain a depth of understanding. When formal assessments are used, truly used, to get a clearer picture of a reader, side by side with authentic, formative data, they add an interesting perspective from which to think about him or her. We keep in mind that although in medicine the diagnosis is often in the story, it is the story that helps the physician know which tests to run. We would not want our doctors to rely solely on what they think the problem is, and we would not want to get a test result without talking to our doctor. We want both from our doctors—formal tests and conversation—to provide the full picture of what is happening for us. This is how assessment should be used with our students.

Our profession is on the verge of one of the biggest changes in our nation's history in terms of education and assessment—the Common Core. "The Common Core State Standards for English Language Arts & Literacy in History/Social Studies, Science, and Technical Subjects ('the Standards') are the culmination of an extended, broad-based effort to fulfill the charge issued by the states to create the next generation of K–12 standards in order to help ensure that all students are college and career ready in literacy no later than the end of high school" (NGA/CCSSO 2010, 3). The Common Core is bringing teachers together nationally to think about what students need to learn and how we will measure that learning. While the Common Core is telling "what" we need to teach our kids, it suggests that we—teachers—need to be the ones to orchestrate "how" we will teach and assess the standards. "The Standards define what all students are expected to know and be able to do, not how teachers should teach. For instance, the use of play with young children is not specified by the Standards, but it is welcome as a valuable activity in its own right and as a way to help students meet the expectations in this document" (NGA/CCSSO 2110, 6).

Over the years we have had our share of new "whats"—what we need to teach, what our district requires, what texts we need to use— but professionally, the "how" of our teaching has always been based on the developmental theory of how children learn. The "how" we teach so our readers can construct their learning. The "how" we teach so our readers have purpose and inquiry. The "how" we teach so our readers run to school. As Debbie Miller reminds us, we have control over "how" we engage our readers in learning. So as we embark on the Common Core standards and the possibility of a national assessment, we will take this opportunity for new learning, and assimilate it with our beliefs in the developmental theory of learning. When we remember what we believe and focus on the act of assessing—the piecing together of the story behind the data available to us—we know we are doing a better job teaching our readers and understanding the process of learning how to read. It is our understanding of children and how they learn that remains a constant for us, and assessment is our window into understanding what each reader needs.

THE STORIES WE CARRY

What Data Are Valued in Our Schools? The Story of a First-Grade Team

A first-grade team is looking over student data in the beginning of the year to determine which students could benefit from extra support in reading. Nina, a classroom teacher on the team, is concerned about one of her students. According to the formal testing data, this student reached the appropriate benchmark on the district assessment and is therefore ineligible for additional support. When Nina confers with him during literacy instruction in the classroom, she is concerned. Nina documents her observations and brings her notes to the meeting to show the intervention team that although the district assessment measures his ability to decode consonant-vowel-consonant (CVC) words well, she is not seeing him understand how to strategically decode unfamiliar words. Her classroom data showed that he is confused about how to use multiple cues to decode and is not remembering the strategies he is learning. Unfortunately, this type of assessment is not considered research based and therefore is not used to determine which students are in need of additional support. Nina's student cannot receive additional support in reading because of his score on the formal test.

When the Numbers Don't Add Up

Joey joined our class as a second grader midyear. His records from his previous school indicated he was at grade level. Our classroom notes from his first few weeks documented that he liked to observe things before trying them. We noted he was reluctant to read aloud to us, so we did not push it at first; according to the records, he was fine. We then tried to get him to talk about his books, but he was vague and often dismissive. Even though he resisted, we started having him read to us, and took notes. We noticed again and again that he lost his place, looked away from the text, and rubbed his eyes. We wondered if perhaps he had a problem with his eyesight. We met with his parents and they took him to the eye doctor, but tests didn't reveal anything wrong. After another month of instruction, taking notes, and watching Joey struggle, we saw he was not progressing toward the goals we had set for him. We reentered the conversation with his parents. Joey was not meeting grade-level benchmarks, something was causing him to struggle, and it did not feel like a reading issue. We administered additional assessments and determined that his reading skills in isolation were fine. His auditory comprehension score was out of sight and his isolated phonetic skills were strong, but when he was presented with small print and many lines, his fluency, accuracy, and comprehension plummeted. He was continuing to slip below benchmark. We asked his parents to please take him back to the eye doctor and tell him our story of Joey in the classroom. In the end, it was revealed that Joey had been legally blind in one eye since birth. He had learned to adapt and pass vision tests by first memorizing the lines with his good eye or tilting his head in such a way that he could still use his good eye when it was covered. Turns out, Joey had no idea you were supposed to see out of both eyes, and we had no idea it was causing him to fall below benchmark as a reader.

CHAPTER 3

Assessment Literacy

When the cook tastes the soup, that's formative: when the guests taste the soup, that's summative.

—Robert Stake, *Assessment as Learning* (2004)

▶ Our district added a new assessment for our students. The Group Reading Assessment and Diagnostic Evaluation (GRADE) was administered to our students twice a year. After the assessment cycle, we received a huge pile of different types of reports. We did not even know how to begin to analyze and interpret the stack of paper in front of us. Our first step was to begin to sort the students by their scores. Some of the scores surprised us. We wanted to understand these students' performances, but we were not familiar enough with the assessment to draw any conclusions. We decided to learn more about the GRADE and determined that it was formal, quantitative, norm-referenced, and diagnostic. New questions then began to emerge: What is norm-referenced? What is a stanine? What areas of reading does it measure? How is this different from our state test? We realized we needed to take some time to understand more about this new assessment before we could begin using it to inform our instructional decisions. ◀

It is not enough to get a number from an assessment; we need to understand that number and how we can use it to teach our readers. When the numbers are surprising or we do not know how to interpret an unfamiliar assessment, it is difficult to know what to do with the information. Before we draw conclusions, it is essential to build our assessment literacy.

Assessment Literacy

Assessment literacy is defined as an understanding of the principles of sound assessment and is present when a person possesses the assessment-related knowledge necessary to interpret and use the information.

—Popham (2009)

When we first heard this term—*assessment literacy*—we loved it! It made perfect sense: we need to build our literacy for assessment or learn how to "read" a particular assessment. When we think about assessment literacy, we like to think about it in the same way we think about literacy in general. When we pick up a piece of text, we know it is essential to ask ourselves some questions: How is this text structured? What is the topic of this text? What is the message or important information in this text? We use the same strategies we use as readers to understand how to read an assessment. Assessment literacy is really no more than building our schema or background knowledge around the different types of assessments we use. Once we have the information we need to read the assessment, we can comprehend and interpret the results. Some assessments require more complex assessment-related knowledge to interpret than others. We need to understand each type of assessment, how it is designed and scored, and how to interpret the varied results so we can use it to understand our readers.

How Is the Assessment Designed?

Assessment tools are grouped into different categories: quantitative or qualitative; diagnostic, formative, or summative; informal or formal. (See Figure 3.1.)

Figure 3.1

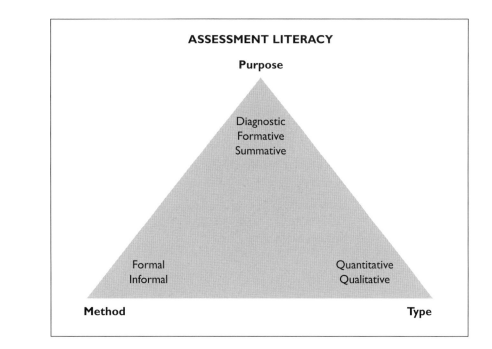

ASSESSMENT LITERACY

Purpose

Diagnostic
Formative
Summative

Formal
Informal

Quantitative
Qualitative

Method

Type

These terms are not really part of our everyday elementary teacher vernacular, so we find it helpful to think about them in the context of how we use them in the classroom. To use the data to help us teach, we have to begin by understanding each assessment through the lens of our practice of teaching reading and ask, "What information can this assessment give me about my students as readers, and how can I use it to help me teach them what they need to learn next?" It is important to understand these assessment tools because each has strengths and limitations in terms of interpretation, and if we are not aware of them, we can draw incorrect conclusions about our readers. We keep the following questions in mind whenever we think about analyzing or understanding the results of an assessment.

What Is My Purpose?

The first category of assessments—diagnostic, formative, and summative—pushes us to think about our purpose for assessing. It is about when and why we are assessing our students. We use diagnostic assessments to provide more in-depth information about a reader. Often we use this type of assessment when we need to get more information to understand why a student is struggling in a particular area of reading. Formative assessments provide us with timely information about what a student is learning and what he or she needs to learn next. These assessments help us plan instruction and monitor a student's progress toward a goal. We use summative assessments to let us know what a student learned from a particular unit of study or after a period of instructional time. Each type has its limitations, so it is important to know when to use each type and how to use the information it provides.

- Do we need a diagnostic, formative, or summative tool?
- When are we giving the assessment and how will we use the information?
- Are we trying to assess our readers before, during, or after a period of instruction?

Diagnostic

Diagnostic assessment is considered a formative assessment, but always occurs before instruction. It looks backward rather than forward. It assesses what learners already know and the nature of any difficulties they might have that, if undiagnosed, might limit their engagement in new learning. It is often used before teaching or when a problem arises. Educators can use a diagnostic assessment (for example, pre-assessments, tests, or self-assessments) to ascertain, before instruction, each student's strengths, weaknesses, knowledge, and skills. Understanding these permits the teacher to adjust the curriculum to meet each student's unique needs.

Formative

Formative assessments are frequent, ongoing, and incorporated into classroom practice so teachers can find the gaps between what students have learned and where they are struggling. They inform both teachers and students about student understanding at a point when timely adjustments can be made. These adjustments help to ensure that students achieve targeted standards-based learning goals within a set time frame. Although formative assessment strategies appear in a variety of formats (such as quizzes, surveys, observations, self-assessments, and student work), they differ from summative assessments in some distinct ways. For instance, formative assessment takes place "in the midst of instruction." Formative assessment helps teachers see what students have learned and determine next steps during the process of learning (Strahan and Rogers 2012).

Summative

Summative assessment is the assessment *of* learning versus assessment *for* learning. A summative assessment typically happens after a specific point in instruction to measure understanding of new learning or to evaluate the effectiveness of instructional programs. These assessments (such as high-stakes tests, standardized state exams, district or interim tests, midterms, and final exams) can be used to check students' mastery of a subject every few weeks or months or some other specified period of time. The goal of summative assessment is to measure the level of success, competency, or proficiency that has been obtained at the end of an instructional phase by comparing it against some standard or benchmark. Summative evaluations can also be used to identify instructional areas that need additional attention.

What Method Should I Use?

The next category of assessments—informal and formal—pushes us to think about our method for assessing. Our informal assessments are designed by us to provide authentic information about how our readers are performing in the classroom. Formal assessments provide data on our students that are valid, reliable, and can be used to compare students. It is helpful to ask these questions:

- Do we need an informal or formal tool?
- How are we administering the assessment, and how can we use the information?
- Do we want to be able to compare our readers with a standard score or do we need an in-depth description of how a reader is performing daily?

Informal

Informal assessments are not data driven, but content and performance driven. Informal assessments can easily be incorporated into classroom routines and learning activities. They can be used at any time without interfering with instructional time. Their results are indicative of the student's competency with the skill or subject of interest. Unlike standardized tests, they are not intended to provide a comparison to a broader group of students. Methods for informal assessment can be divided into two main types: unstructured (such as student work samples and journals) and structured (such as checklists and observations). The unstructured methods frequently are somewhat more difficult to score and evaluate, but they can provide a great deal of valuable information about children's skills. Structured methods can be reliable and valid techniques when time is spent creating the "scoring" procedures. Informal assessment is limited, because we cannot use it to compare a student to a large population and it does not have the statistical reliability to draw conclusions about one student in comparison to other students his or her age.

Formal

Formal assessment typically means using a test that involves standardized administration and that has norms and a formal interpretive procedure. We usually refer to these types of tests as standardized measures (for example, tests, quizzes, and papers). Formal assessments have data that support the conclusions drawn from the test. These tests have been tried before on students and have statistics that support their outcomes, such as the conclusion that a student's reading is below average for his or her age. Formal assessments are used to assess overall achievement, to compare a student's performance with others at his or her age or grade, or to identify comparable strengths and weaknesses with peers. The data are mathematically computed and summarized. Scores such as percentiles, stanines, or standard scores are most commonly given from this type of assessment. Formal assessments are designed to allow us to easily interpret and draw conclusions about a student's performance, but we need to keep in mind that even a formal assessment provides only a snapshot of information about a student. That information may be limited because of the number of questions on the assessment that measured a particular area or skill. For example, if a student ranks at a low percentile in understanding poetry, but there was only one question on poetry, we need to be careful about drawing conclusions based on this one assessment.

It is the formal assessments that typically push us out of our comfort zone in terms of assessment literacy. In elementary schools, we typically find two types of formal assessments: standards-based and norm–referenced. Each is designed differently and therefore is scored and interpreted differently. There are some important terms to keep in mind when thinking about these formal assessments. We have found that we need to have a deep understanding of these terms and how these assessments are designed in order to understand the results and talk with families about a student's performance. Figure 3.2 provides definitions for some important terms we keep in mind when analyzing these types of formal assessments.

What Type of Data Do I Need?

The quantitative and qualitative categories push us to think about the type of data we need. It is about whether we want to get a numerical score or measure on our students or a more in-depth description of how they are learning. The following questions help us decide:

- Do we need a quantitative or qualitative tool?

- *Standards-Based Assessment:* A standards-based test measures how a student performs against a specified set of standards. The test does not compare the student to another group of students but measures how much a student knows about a particular standard. Typically a standards-based assessment has three to four different performance levels. Some examples of standards-based assessments include many state tests (such as the New England Common Assessment Program, or NECAP), the much anticipated Common Core assessment (Partnership for Assessment of Readiness for College and Careers, or PARCC) or Smarter Balanced Assessment Consortium (SBAC), and Standards-Based Report Cards.
- *Norm-Referenced Assessment:* "Norm-referenced tests allow us to compare a student's skills to others in his age group. Norm-referenced tests are developed by creating the test items and then administering the test to a group of students that will be used as the basis of comparison. Statistical methods are used to determine how raw scores will be interpreted and what performance levels are assigned to each score." (Logsdon 2012). Some examples of norm-referenced tests are the GRADE, the Stanford, and the Dynamic Indicators of Basic Early Literacy Skills (DIBELS).
- *Percentile Rank:* Percentile rank is one score that is typically shown on a norm-referenced test. It compares one student's score with the scores of a similar group of students. If a student scores at the fifty-sixth percentile on a norm-referenced test, that means the student has scored as well as or better than 56 percent of students his or her age from the normative sample of the test.
- *Stanine:* A stanine is a standardized student score that is often used to report scores on a norm-referenced test. Stanines range from 1 to 9 with a standard deviation of 2. In general, stanines of 1 to 3 are considered below average, stanines of 4 to 6 are considered average, and stanines of 7 to 9 are considered above average. A difference of 2 between the stanines for two measures indicates that the two measures are significantly different. Stanines, like percentiles, indicate a student's relative standing in a norm group.
- *Raw Score:* The raw score is the number of items answered correctly on a given test. For example, if a test had fifty-nine items and the student got twenty-three correct, the raw score would be 23. Raw scores by themselves have little or no meaning. Raw scores are converted to (1) developmental scores such as grade equivalents or (2) status scores such as percentile rank, normal curve equivalents, or stanines in order to be interpreted meaningfully.
- *Grade Equivalent (GE):* The GE is a score reported on norm-referenced tests that allows educators and parents to compare students based on the performance of other students relative to the school year. Assuming a nine-month school year (typically September through May), the score represents a period during the year and is displayed as a number to show a grade and a month. The score is an estimate of the performance that an average student at a particular grade level is assumed to demonstrate on the test at a particular time in the school year. For example, a score of 5.8 represents a performance level typical of fifth-grade students in the eighth month (April) of the school year.
- *Performance Level:* This term refers to four levels of performance on a state standards-based exam (such as advanced, proficient, needs improvement, and warning/failure). Performance levels have a cut score to designate each level and a description of the skills and knowledge a student must have demonstrated on the test to have scored at a particular performance level.

Figure 3.2
Important Terms in Assessment

- What kind of information are we collecting, and how can we use it?
- Are we assessing a student's fluency rate or instructional level or do we need information on the quality of his or her strategy use?

Quantitative

Quantitative methods are those that focus on numbers, amounts, and frequencies rather than on meaning and experience. Quantitative methods (such as questionnaires, psychometric tests, high-stakes tests, and standardized state exams) provide information that is easy to analyze statistically and is fairly reliable. The data are mathematically computed and summarized. Scores such as percentiles, stanines, or standard scores are most commonly derived from this type of assessment. Quantitative methods are associated with the scientific and experimental approach, and these kinds of assessments provide us with a number by which to measure a reader. This number often tells us whether a student is performing securely, independently, or inadequately. The number helps us quickly get a sense of how a student is doing and provides information that is easy to analyze. Quantitative assessments have their limitations because they do not provide the in-depth descriptions that qualitative assessments do.

Qualitative

Qualitative methods are ways of collecting data that are concerned with describing meaning rather than with drawing statistical inferences. Qualitative methods aim to gather an in-depth understanding of human behavior and the reasons that govern such behavior. The qualitative method investigates the *why* and *how* of a behavior, not just *what, where*, and *when*. What qualitative methods (such as case studies, observations, and interviews) lose in reliability they gain in validity. They provide a more in-depth and rich description.

Both types of assessment have limitations, but they complement each other beautifully. A running record is a great example of how quantitative and qualitative data complement each other. Take a look at Kate's running record (Figure 3.3).

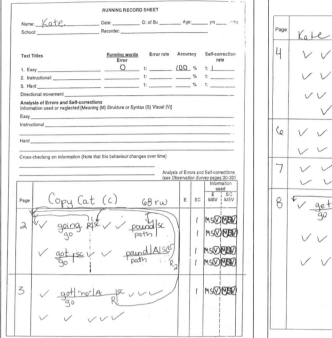

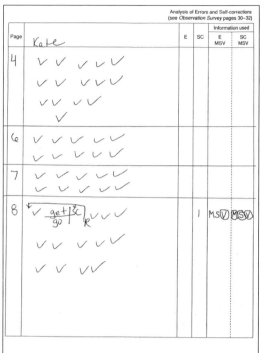

Figure 3.3

Kate's running record is a powerful example of using both quantitative data and qualitative data to understand a reader. If we had calculated only the number, it would have seemed that Level C was too easy for Kate. The qualitative data show us that she had many opportunities for instruction at this level. The amount of rereading and self-correcting she had to do did not make this a smooth read for her. We also noticed that after all the reading work she had to do, she was not able to comprehend what happened in the story. Because we analyzed the qualitative data, we knew Kate needed to look through the whole word and not guess based on the first letter cue. We also needed to teach Kate that it helps readers to think about what they are reading as they read so that they can remember the story and talk about it with others. In this case, the percentage of accuracy—or the quantitative number—gave us only a piece of the information. The qualitative data gave us the in-depth information we needed to understand the quality of her accurate reading.

Assessments Can Fall Under More Than One Category

Although assessment tools are grouped into different categories, these categories are not mutually exclusive. One assessment tool can fall into more than one category, as the following examples show:

- An assessment can be diagnostic (given before instruction occurs); formal (provides data that have statistics to support the conclusion); and quantitative (provides data that focus on numbers). The Northwest Evaluation Association (NWEA), GRADE, and Stanford 10 are examples of assessments that fall into all of these categories.

- An assessment can be quantitative (provides data that focus on numbers); qualitative (provides an in-depth description); informal (provides data on how a student is performing on classroom content); and formative (provides data on what a student needs to learn next based on how they are performing during instruction). A running record is a good example.

- An assessment can be summative (provides data on what a student has learned after a period of instruction); formal (provides data that have statistics to support the conclusion); and quantitative (provides data that focus on numbers). Many state tests fall into these categories.

As you look at Figure 3.4, you will notice that our purpose in using an assessment can cause it to be defined differently. The same tool can be diagnostic, formative, or summative, depending on when and how we use it. Following are some examples.

Running Record

In Figure 3.4, we show how a running record can be categorized as a diagnostic, formative, or summative assessment. If we are using a running record as a pre-assessment to look backward and assess what the reader already knows, then the running record is diagnostic. We are using the information to understand a student's strengths and weaknesses so we can plan instruction. Once we begin instruction, we use ongoing, intermittent running records as a formative assessment to see how a reader is applying the strategies we are teaching during instructional sessions. This helps us see what the reader knows as she practices what she is learning in an authentic context to help us determine what she needs to learn next. If we use a running record at the end of a marking period or instructional unit to measure the level of success, competency, or proficiency that has been obtained at the end of this instructional phase and compare a student's score against some standard or benchmark, then it is summative. This running record is now a measure of what the student has learned as a result of instruction.

Figure 3.4 Taking a Look at Some Elementary Reading Assessments

Name of Assessment	Formal	Informal	Qualitative	Quantitative	Diagnostic	Formative	Summative
State Test	☑			☑	☑		☑
TerraNova, Third Edition Multiple Assessments	☑			☑	☑		☑
Group Reading Assessment and Diagnostic Evaluation (GRADE)	☑			☑	☑		☑
Northwest Evaluation Association (NWEA)	☑			☑	☑		☑
Stanford Achievement Test Series, Tenth Edition (Stanford 10)	☑			☑	☑		☑
Developmental Reading Assessment, Second Edition (DRA2)	☑		☑	☑	☑	☑	☑
Fountas and Pinnell Benchmark Assessment System (BAS)	☑		☑	☑	☑	☑	☑
Qualitative Reading Inventory, Fourth Edition (QRI-4)		☑	☑	☑	☑	☑	☑
Teachers College Fiction Reading Assessments		☑	☑	☑	☑	☑	☑
Teachers College Common-Core-Aligned Performance Assessments		☑	☑		☑		☑
Observation Survey	☑		☑	☑	☑	☑	☑
Running Records		☑	☑	☑	☑	☑	☑
Reading Conference Notes		☑	☑			☑	
Student Self-Reflection		☑	☑		☑	☑	☑
High-Frequency Word List		☑	☑	☑	☑	☑	☑
Student Work (Book Logs, Writing Samples)		☑	☑		☑	☑	☑

These assessments can be used as diagnostic, formative, and summative assessments because they can be given multiple times during the year:
- Diagnostic—Analyzed to understand what a learner already knows before instruction
- Formative—Analyzed to plan upcoming instruction
- Summative—Measure of whether or not a student is meeting grade-level benchmarks

Figure 3.4 Taking a Look at Some Elementary Reading Assessments *(continued)*

Name of Assessment	Formal	Informal	Qualitative	Quantitative	Diagnostic	Formative	Summative
Consortium on Reading Excellence (CORE) Phonics Survey		✓	✓	✓	✓	✓	✓
Consortium on Reading Excellence (CORE) Phoneme Segmentation and Deletion Tests		✓	✓	✓	✓	✓	
Consortium on Reading Excellence (CORE) Graded High-Frequency Word Survey		✓	✓	✓	✓	✓	✓
Words Their Way Spelling Inventories	✓		✓	✓	✓	✓	
Phonological Awareness Skills Text (PAST)		✓	✓		✓	✓	
Lexia Quick Reading Test	✓		✓	✓	✓	✓	✓
Names Assessment		✓	✓	✓	✓		
Quick Phonics Screener		✓	✓	✓	✓	✓	✓
Dynamic Indicator of Basic Early Literacy Skills (DIBELS)	✓			✓			✓
AIMSweb	✓			✓			✓

The DIBELS and AIMSweb are universal screeners (refer to page 40). These assessments help us identify which students may be at-risk of academic failure but they do not help us understand *why* a student is struggling. Therefore we did not place a check ☑ in the diagnostic box.

Student Self-Reflection

A self-reflection can also be a diagnostic, formative, or summative assessment, depending on when we collect the information and how we use it. If we ask students to write a self-reflection on what they do well as readers and what they like to read at the beginning of the school year, the self-reflection is diagnostic. The information we glean from this initial self-reflection helps us understand a student's strengths and weaknesses before we even begin teaching. Once we begin instruction, we introduce our students to new genres and authors and teach them new strategies for monitoring for meaning as they read. We then use intermittent self-reflections to assess how the student is trying to apply these new strategies. Even though the questions on the self-reflection may be the same as or similar to those on the diagnostic self-reflection at the beginning of the year, we now treat it as a formative assessment. We use the information to help us understand what the student has learned, and we alter our upcoming instruction accordingly. At the end of the unit, we also ask our students to write a final self-reflection, but this time it acts as a summative assessment. The goal of the end-of-unit self-reflection is to measure what students have learned over the course of that instructional phase.

State Test

A state test can also be a diagnostic or summative assessment, depending on when we choose to analyze the data. When we look at the prior year's state test results for the students who will be in our classrooms in September, the test acts as a diagnostic assessment. Looking at the data of our future students shows us which ones did not pass the state test, meaning we will need to reassess them in September. We can also look at the data of our upcoming students to see if there are particular standards, skills, or concepts that 70 percent or more had difficulty mastering. Looking at the data in this way helps us identify some of the concepts we need to teach over the course of the school year.

The state test is a summative assessment when we analyze the results of the students that we taught in the instructional year it was administered. These results show each student's level of proficiency according to the state standards. The results help us evaluate the effectiveness of our instructional program and identify students who may need additional support in the upcoming year. When we use it as a summative measure, we can evaluate which question types were missed most frequently and identify areas of the curriculum to enhance.

Voices from the Classroom
Building Assessment Literacy

State Test

The state test results are in! I come into school to find a huge pile of paper on my desk. "What is all of this? When will I have time to even look at it?" By midday I can't stand having the pile on my desk so I begin to sort through it during lunch. (When else does a teacher have a minute to think?) I know the test is a summative, formal, quantitative assessment. As I look through the reports, I notice that some have particular items highlighted or have columns with specific abbreviations that I do not understand. I start to write down the questions I generate as I look through the data:

Which questions did less than 75 percent of the students answer accurately?

How can I find out which questions the students missed?

Which standards correspond to those questions?

What are the actual questions?

Were the questions multiple-choice or open-response questions?

Is there a particular type of question or genre that students struggled to answer correctly?

How do I identify a pattern of errors on this assessment that helps me identify a concept or skill I need to add to my current curriculum?

I have a lot of questions to answer about how this test is designed before I can begin to draw any conclusions. Maybe we can use our next grade-level team meeting to talk about the assessment, I think to myself.

Running Records

I love the week before school begins. The classroom is ready—everything labeled and in its place. I still get butterflies in my stomach from the anticipation of meeting twenty-five new friends. "Okay," I tell myself. "The plan for today is to look through my students' year-end running records so I can start thinking about which books I will introduce and plan possible strategy groups." I get a cup of tea and settle in. "What are all these letters and circles?" I ask myself as I flip through several running records. I have never seen a running record with all these *Ms, Ss,* and *Vs.* "What do they mean? I always just count the errors, calculate the level, and call it a day." The more I look at the running records, the more I begin to think maybe I am missing something. I understand what this assessment is telling me about the quantitative level—both instructional and independent—for my readers. Maybe I need to spend some time learning how to analyze the qualitative data on the strategies a reader uses when he or she reaches a point of difficulty. I do not know how to use this assessment to determine a reader's areas of strengths and weaknesses. I will put that on the never ending "To Do list" for later this week! ◄

What Area of Reading Does
the Assessment Measure?

It is not enough for us to understand how assessments are designed, scored, and administered. We also need to understand exactly what an assessment is measuring in terms of reading. We have found that in our work to build our assessment literacy, we also end up building our "literacy literacy." We have come to know more about each area of reading and to truly understand how each area works to develop effective, efficient readers. In the area of reading, the research highlights six areas to measure: phonemic awareness, accuracy, comprehension, fluency, vocabulary, and reading disposition. (See Figure 3.5.)

Figure 3.5
Six Areas of
Reading

To fully understand what a reader knows and what she needs to learn, we assess her knowledge in all six areas of reading:

- *Phonemic Awareness:* This describes a reader's ability to focus on and manipulate phonemes in spoken words.
- *Accuracy:* This refers to a reader's ability to use her knowledge of the visual information to read the words in the text accurately. When we assess a student's accuracy, we look at her knowledge of phonics, what she understands about the concepts about print, and her knowledge of high-frequency words. We want to understand which isolated skills a reader knows, and how she uses these same skills when reading authentic text.
  - *Phonics:* The National Reading Panel defines phonics as "a reader's knowledge of how letters correspond to sounds and how to use this knowledge in reading and spelling" (2000).
  - *Concepts About Print:* This describes an emergent reader's understanding of important print concepts, such as understanding how books are read (left to right), identifying pictures versus words, knowing the difference between a letter and a word, and identifying punctuation marks.
  - *High-Frequency Words:* This category explores a reader's ability to read the most frequently used words in the English language. Many of the high-frequency words cannot be decoded and must be memorized.
- *Fluency:* This refers to a reader's ability to read accurately, smoothly, expressively, and at an appropriate rate.
- *Comprehension:* The National Reading Panel says comprehension is "a reader's ability to understand what she read. Comprehension is an active process that requires an intentional and thoughtful interaction between the reader and the text" (2000).
- *Vocabulary:* Reading Rockets describes this area of reading as "a reader's use and knowledge of the words in order to communicate effectively. There are four types of vocabulary: listening, speaking, reading, and writing. Listening vocabulary refers to the words we need to know to understand what we hear. Speaking vocabulary consists of the words we use when we speak. Reading vocabulary refers to the words we need to know to understand what we read. Writing vocabulary consists of the words we use in writing" (2013).
- *Reading Disposition:* A reader's disposition is how a student feels about herself as a reader. It measures how much time a student spends reading, what she likes to read, what she feels she needs to learn, and how confident and competent she feels about her own skills.

Whenever we come across a new assessment, we take the time to figure out which areas of reading it measures. That helps us focus our attention and think about our readers' strengths and weaknesses. Many assessment tools measure more than one area of reading (Figure 3.6). Here are some examples:

- The Developmental Reading Assessment 2 (DRA2) measures accuracy, comprehension, fluency, and disposition.
- The CORE Literacy Library is composed of many different assessments that measure different areas of reading. The CORE Phonics Survey measures a student's knowledge of isolated phonics skills. The CORE Phonological and Phoneme Tests measure phonemic awareness, and the CORE Graded High-Frequency Word Survey measures a student's knowledge of sight words. There are also assessments to measure encoding, vocabulary, fluency, and comprehension in the CORE Literacy Library.
- The DIBELS Nonsense Word Fluency screens accuracy (phonics), the Phoneme Segmentation Fluency screens phonemic awareness, and the Initial Sound Fluency screens phonemic awareness.
- The GRADE measures comprehension and vocabulary.
- The Fountas and Pinnell Benchmark Assessment System measures accuracy, comprehension, and fluency. (There are also assessments in the system that measure phonemic awareness, phonics, vocabulary, and disposition.)

Even when we have enough assessment literacy to understand what a number means, we still need to understand its effects on how we teach reading. Our assessment literacy coupled with our "literacy literacy" helps us form diagnoses for our readers and understand why they are struggling. For us, it is not enough just to know they are struggling; we need to know why they are struggling so we can provide intervention that meets their specific needs as readers. In some schools, the intervention model is "one size fits all." Students who are struggling get the same program regardless of diagnosis. For example, we have seen students in an intervention that is based only on decoding, even though they need support in inferential thinking. We need to make sure that our struggling readers are receiving the appropriate instruction and that the tools we are using to monitor progress

Figure 3.6 Areas of Reading Measured on Frequently Used Elementary Reading Assessments

Name of Assessment	Phonemic Awareness	Accuracy (Phonics, High-Frequency Words, Concepts About Print)	Comprehension	Fluency	Vocabulary	Disposition/ Metacognition
State Test			✓		✓	
TerraNova, Third Edition Multiple Assessments			✓		✓	
Group Reading Assessment and Diagnostic Evaluation (GRADE)	✓	✓	✓		✓	
Northwest Evaluation Association (NWEA)	✓	✓	✓		✓	
Stanford Achievement Test Series, Tenth Edition (Stanford 10)	✓	✓	✓		✓	
Developmental Reading Assessment, Second Edition (DRA2)	✓	✓	✓	✓		✓
Fountas and Pinnell Benchmark Assessment System (BAS)	✓	✓	✓	✓	✓	✓
Qualitative Reading Inventory, Fourth Edition (QRI-4)		✓	✓			
Teachers College Fiction Reading Assessments		✓	✓	✓		
Teachers College Common-Core-Aligned Performance Assessments			✓			
Observation Survey		✓		✓		
Running Records		✓		✓		
Reading Conference Notes (☑ depends on the questions asked.)		✓	✓	✓	✓	✓
Student Self-Reflection						✓
High-Frequency Word List		✓				
Student Work (Book Logs, Writing Samples) (☑ depends on the type of student work.)		✓	✓	✓	✓	✓

Figure 3.6 Areas of Reading Measured on Frequently Used Elementary Reading Assessments *(continued)*

Name of Assessment	Phonemic Awareness	Accuracy (Phonics, High-Frequency Words, Concepts About Print)	Comprehension	Fluency	Vocabulary	Disposition/ Metacognition
Consortium on Reading Excellence (CORE) Phonics Survey		☑				
Consortium on Reading Excellence (CORE) Phonological and Phoneme Tests	☑	☑				
Consortium on Reading Excellence (CORE) Graded High-Frequency Word Survey		☑				
Words Their Way Spelling Inventories		☑ (Encoding only)				
Phonological Awareness Skills Text (PAST)	☑					
Lexia Quick Reading Test		☑				
Names Assessment		☑				
Quick Phonics Screener		☑				
Dynamic Indicator of Basic Early Literacy Skills (DIBELS)	☑	☑		☑ (Reading Rate)		
AIMSweb	☑	☑	☑	☑ (Reading Rate)		

are monitoring the area of reading we are targeting. If students are receiving intervention on using strategies to decode effectively but are being assessed on fluency rate to monitor progress, then we have no idea how they are actually progressing in their strategy application. The assessment tool and the instruction do not correlate and therefore will not give us a true picture of how this reader is progressing in the targeted area. It is important that we understand what a tool measures and know that it will actually monitor the progress of what we are teaching.

The concept of "literacy literacy" has really helped us become better teachers of reading. As we learn more about an assessment, we begin to ask more questions of ourselves as teachers of reading. These questions push us to learn more about an aspect of reading and how to teach it better. Recent advances in technology have allowed the research on reading to become more and more specific. We know more now than we ever have about the human brain and what a reader actually does to decode and comprehend text. Assessment has been a doorway into our continued professional learning about the process of reading and how to best support our struggling readers.

New Terms in Assessment

Response to Intervention (RTI) legislation has pushed us to build our assessment literacy in new ways. This legislation has generated some requirements in terms of how, when, and the frequency with which we assess our students. These requirements are mandated, and we teachers do not have much control over some of the assessments we now have to use. The quantitative and formal nature of many of these required assessments makes it even more important for us to make sure we understand the design of the assessment tool, what area of reading it assesses, and how the scores can be interpreted. Here are the definitions and implications of some important new terms.

> *Common Assessments:* Common assessments are assessments that all teachers in a given grade level or school are required to administer to identified students at specific times of the year. Common assessments may be brief (such as DIBELS) or more extensive (such as the Fountas and Pinnell Benchmark Assessment System). These common assessments could fall into all of the categories we discussed earlier in this chapter: quantitative or qualitative; diagnostic, formative, or summative; informal or formal. The fact that all teachers are giving the assessment in the same manner and that it is required makes it a common assessment. (See Figures 3.7 and 3.8.)
>
> *Curriculum-Based Measurement:* Curriculum-based measurement, or CBM, is a common assessment used to monitor student educational progress through direct assessment of academic skills. CBMs are typically brief, timed samples, or "probes," made up of academic material taken from the child's school curriculum. Many CBMs are screeners and used for progress monitoring in relationship to RTI.

Figure 3.7
Common
Assessments:
The
Opportunities

Common assessments cause a lot of frustration among elementary educators because they are mandated, and we do not always believe they provide the best information about our readers because they are often quantitative and formal. Although frustrating, they also provide a lot of opportunities when they are used appropriately. "Common assessments are the essential engine for continual improvement" (Schmoker 2011, 70). Common assessments give us an opportunity to work as a grade level, school, district, or state.

When we have a common tool, we can focus our time and professional dialogue on understanding exactly what the assessment measures and the type of information it can give us. We also think it is important to recognize that common assessments, because of their formal nature, provide a different type of information about our students. The data tell us how our students performed on a measure in relation to many other students their age.

Figure 3.8
The Common
Core: The
Common
Assessment?

The Common Core State Standards are the first step toward one or two possible national common assessments:

Like adoption of common core standards, it will be up to the states: some states plan to come together voluntarily to develop a common assessment system, based on the common core state standards. A state-led consortium on assessment would be grounded in the following principles: allow for comparison across students, schools, districts, states and nations; create economies of scale; provide information and support more effective teaching and learning; and prepare students for college and careers. (Common Core State Standards Initiative)

The Department of Education has put $350 million into two groups— Partnership for Assessment of Readiness for College and Careers (PARCC) and Smarter Balanced Assessment Consortium (SBAC)—to develop standardized tests that can be given across participating states. The plan is for these assessments to be taken on computers and for them to focus on higher-level thinking, reading, and writing skills. In terms of assessment literacy, it is most likely that these tools will be formal, summative, and quantitative. Lucy Calkins discusses this topic in the book *Pathways to the Common Core*:

[We] are sure to have lots of question about these assessments. Will there be one national test? Will it be internationally benchmarked? Will it be scored centrally? Will state results be announced against a comparison group composed of students in that state or students in all states within PARCC's or SBAC's reach? Many of the answers to your questions (and ours) are not available yet—and the answers that are available keep changing. For now, educators must wait to see what will come from the effort to create new Common Core–aligned assessments. (2012, 189–190)

Universal Screeners: The National Center on Response to Intervention (NCRTI) defines universal screening as brief assessments that are valid and reliable, and that demonstrate diagnostic accuracy for predicting which students will develop learning or behavioral problems. They are conducted with all students to identify those who are at-risk of academic failure and, therefore, need more intensive intervention.

Progress Monitoring: NCRTI defines student progress monitoring as repeated measurement of performance to inform the instruction of individual students in general and special education in grades K–8. These tools must be reliable and valid for representing students' development and have demonstrated utility for helping teachers plan more effective instruction. Progress monitoring is conducted at least monthly to

- estimate rates of improvement;
- identify students who are not demonstrating adequate progress; and
- compare the efficacy of different forms of instruction to design more effective, individualized instruction.

Performance Assessments: Teachers College Reading and Writing Project (2010) suggests using performance assessments to engage students in authentic, high-level work that is aligned to curricular standards. Using authentic work to assess allows teachers to carefully plan instruction that meets students where they are and truly moves them forward. These assessments can be used as both pre- and post-assessments.

Voices from the Classroom
Building Assessment Literacy

Why Do We Need a Common Assessment?

We planned a meeting with all the kindergarten teachers across the district to talk about the assessments they were giving. Each team had their own "homegrown" assessments that they liked, and they weren't interested in changing to a common assessment. As district coaches, we were finding it really difficult to analyze all these different assessments and try to make decisions around support for readers. We began the meeting with each team sharing what tools they were using to assess and why. After each team shared, it was clear they all agreed on which areas of literacy they should be assessing, but each preferred the tool they were using.

"It would really help us if you could all agree on one tool to assess Letter Identification, Concepts about Print, and Sight Words. It is difficult to have so many tools. It seems you all are assessing these areas, but with different tools," Tammy said.

Robin replied, "Why do we have to do that? We have always used these, and they work. Why does it matter what another school or teacher uses? I need to know what I need to know."

"For your formative data we totally agree—it doesn't matter. But now we are trying to look at the data across the district to make decisions on resources and supports for students. It makes it difficult for us to make these types of analyses and comparisons if you are all measuring in different ways. Does that make sense?" asked Tammy.

Robin said, "I can see how it makes sense for you, but it does not make sense for us in terms of classroom use. Many of us will have to learn a new tool."

"You're right. But now we are using the data for more than one purpose. We don't want to assess them twice, so we were hoping to agree on one tool so that we can all use the data," Tammy explained.

"It makes sense, but I don't want to learn a new tool. I like the one I use—I am sure everyone prefers the one they use," replied Robin.

Heather asked, "How will we choose which one?"

"We can figure that all out together," Tammy assured her. "We know everyone will not necessarily agree, but we want to make sure everyone understands why we need a common measure."

What Is a Screener?

A team of kindergarten teachers was reviewing their midyear data.

"Why are we giving two different assessments on Letter ID? Do we really need to assess that twice?" The district common assessment plan required the administration of the DIBELS Letter-Naming subtest and the Letter-ID assessment from Marie Clay's *An Observation Survey* (1993).

"The DIBELS was added two years ago. We should talk with Kathy and find out why the district needs us to give two Letter ID assessments. We are already overassessing these kids; it would be great to get rid of one of them."

The next week the team set up a meeting with Kathy, the district literacy coach, to discuss the Letter ID assessments.

After hearing the concerns, Kathy said, "The DIBELS is a diagnostic screener and measures a student's ability to rapidly name letters. The Letter ID is not a predictive screener and measures a student's knowledge of all the letters in the alphabet. The DIBELS is a timed assessment and the focus is on both knowledge of letters and processing speed. The Letter ID is not timed, so the focus is on letter knowledge. Each assessment really serves a different purpose."

"Isn't it more important to just know which letters they know? Why do we need it timed?" asked Julie.

"Well, the Marie Clay is definitely better as a formative assessment. The DIBELS serves a different purpose as a screener, and we need a screener for RTI," Kathy replied.

"Jargon, jargon!" Jen exclaimed. "Explain."

"A screener is just a quick test that has been designed to predict if students will have a learning issue. It has been designed to be valid and reliable. It does not tell you what a student needs to learn, but will highlight a student of concern. We need to have a screener for RTI as one piece of data to make grouping decisions and measure progress," explained Kathy.

"So it is not supposed to really help us know what to teach?" asked Julie.

"No," Kathy replied.

"That's good because it doesn't," said Julie. "At least now we know why we are giving it and the purpose of the screener." ◄

Assessment literacy is about building our understanding of assessment and how to use it to teach reading effectively. Maya Angelou said, "We do best with what we know, and when we know better, we do better." Assessment literacy is about knowing better. It provides us with the knowledge to approach assessment with a stance of purpose, inquiry, and understanding. When we use assessment this way, we are always one step closer to finding the stories of our readers.

THE STORIES WE CARRY

What Does the Assessment Really Tell Me?

Mindy stacked the chairs, turned off her computer, packed up her things, and headed for the district inservice meeting. She had ten minutes to get across town for the meeting. Maybe enough time to grab a coffee and a granola bar on the way—she had called a parent during lunch and never ate. She found a parking space and made her way into the cafeteria. She tried to fit comfortably onto the bench while ignoring the sticky residue on the table and the stale smell of tacos in the air. The lights went down, the PowerPoint went up, and the next sixty minutes consisted of a slide show of the data and what felt like a lecture on how the district was not meeting standards. The audience filed out in silence, and Mindy left feeling overwhelmed and stressed.

The next day, Cyndy, Mindy's principal, used the grade-level team time to talk about the district meeting. Cyndy had created displays to look at how their students in grade four had performed on the state test over the past four years. She explained how the test was designed and the different types of questions on the test. As they looked at their data, they quickly noticed that their students' performance had actually improved in one question type and worsened in the other question type over the past four years. The students were doing better on multiple-choice questions; it was the open-response questions that seemed to be a problem. Mindy and her team were surprised by these results. They had been teaching students to write responses to literature during interactive read-aloud and reading workshop. The students had also done this type of writing in third grade and were clearly used to writing in this format when they began the school year. The team decided to get more information to understand what was going on. They planned to get the state rubrics and exemplars for the open-response questions and bring them to their next meeting along with the students' reading notebooks.

At the next meeting, Clare joined the team to look at the test passages, the open-response questions, the rubric, and the exemplars for each question on the test. They took the time to understand exactly what these types of questions were assessing. They noticed that the state was not only looking for the correct answer with supporting evidence, but that students needed to include an explanation to receive full credit for their answer. They then looked at their students' scores. Most students were receiving two out of four full points, which indicated that they were not always including enough evidence or an explanation to support how the evidence answered the questions. They looked at the students' notebooks and noticed that the chart they were using to record their thinking did not include a section for the explanation. Most notebook responses were accurate but had only one piece of supporting evidence and no explanation. Looking at the data and taking the time to build both their assessment literacy and "literacy literacy" gave the team the information they needed to influence instruction.

CHAPTER 4

Triangulating Assessment

> *Despite my training in measurement, I have come to regard normative, stan-dardized tests as having a place in education, but as indirect ways of informing teachers about learning. They need to be supplemented at the classroom level with systematic observations of children who are in the act of responding to instruction.*
>
> —Marie Clay, *An Observation Survey* (1993)

▶ Zachary was a kindergarten student in Ms. Frasier's class. Ms. Frasier's district assessment plan required every kindergarten student to draw a self-portrait each week for the first month of school. Figure 4.1 shows Zachary's first and second self-portraits. If the dates on these portraits were reversed, we would all think Ms. Frasier qualified for teacher of the year; the parent talk on the soccer field sidelines would have been, "You have to have Ms. Frasier for your kindergarten teacher—she works wonders!" Unfortunately, like most things in a classroom full of young friends, it does not work out that easily or neatly. Teaching and assessing are messy!

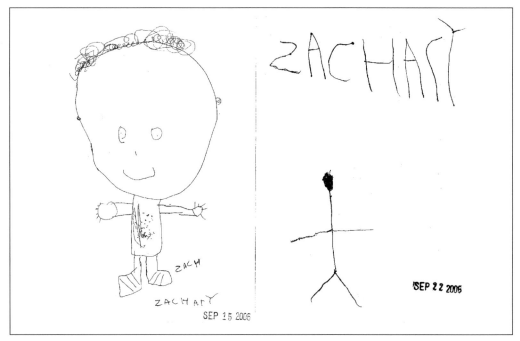

Figure 4.1
Zachary's Self-Portraits

If the teacher were to look only at Zachary's self-portrait from September 22, she would have real concerns about his fine-motor abilities. Looking at these two data points, however, left Ms. Frasier with some authentic questions: Did he break his arm? Use the wrong hand while drawing? Is he having self-esteem issues? Did he put his name on someone else's drawing? Have I managed to ruin him in only three weeks of school? Ms. Frasier took a deep breath and began to find the explanation.

She looked at her conferring notes. On September 15, Zachary was quite capable of drawing a detailed self-portrait. She then dug deeper and took a look at other drawing samples from Zachary. They all looked more like the September 15 sample. Whew—she had not ruined him! She then looked at her conferring notes and noticed he was in the block area on September 22 before he was called to do his weekly self-portrait assessment. She decided to talk with him about his drawing to get better insights about why he drew his self-portrait differently on September 22. Zachary assured Ms. Frasier that nothing monumental had happened to the developmental trajectory of his fine-motor abilities or his self-esteem. It seems that when it was his turn for the assessment, he and his friends had just finished building a castle in the block area. The knights were about to storm the castle to defend the king and rescue the queen. He did not want to miss this exciting event (honestly, how often do kindergarten students even get to use blocks anymore?), so he finished his self-portrait as quickly as possible and returned to blocks for the big event. ◀

We know this is a simple example, but we find it simple enough (and funny enough) to remind us to always triangulate our data to find the stories of our readers. Triangulating data is defined as using multiple sources of data to illuminate, confirm, or dispute what you learned from an initial analysis of one piece of data:

> When triangulating sources, it can be helpful to draw on different types of assessments (quantitative or qualitative and formal or informal), on assessments taken at different intervals (diagnostic, formative, or summative), and to look for both patterns and inconsistencies across student responses to the assessments. (Boudett, City, and Murnane 2005, 90–91)

When we think about assessment in terms of digging deeper and piecing together parts to understand a whole, we are using what we "know for sure" about teaching and learning, and the role of assessment in both (see Chapter 2). By definition, when we triangulate, we never define a reader by a number. Triangulating brings to life what we know for sure—the importance of moving beyond the number and using assessment to design classroom experiences to observe our readers in the process of learning so we can understand what each reader needs.

The different categories of assessment tools we described in Chapter 3 give us opportunities to triangulate our data. (See Figure 3.1.) These various tools provide different types of data and data at different intervals so we can triangulate the information we have about our readers. Let's take a look at Zachary for a minute. Zachary's data are triangulated because he drew a self-portrait four times (at different intervals). This provides data points taken at different intervals so we can look for patterns or inconsistencies over time. There was a pattern in Zachary's self-portraits that did not make sense. Ms. Frasier further triangulated her data by looking at other drawing samples from Zachary during this time frame, by looking at her classroom notes to remember what was happening in the classroom when he did his self-portrait, and by talking with Zachary about his self-portraits. Although these all fall into the informal category, they are different sources of informal data. She used multiple data points to answer the questions she had about the inconsistencies she was seeing in his self-portraits. Triangulating was the means to revealing the story behind these drawings and Zachary's fine-motor skills.

When we triangulate, we get multiple pieces of data on a student, and each piece of data pushes us to ask more questions and get more data to answer these questions. (See Figure 4.2.)

Sometimes we may have only one source of data, and the first step of triangulating is getting more. Our purpose, or what we want to know about a reader, helps us determine what additional information we need to understand that reader. Our assessment literacy helps us understand which tools will give us the type of information we need, and what we know about literacy helps us understand which area of reading to assess. (See Chapter 3 for more information on assessment literacy and "literacy literacy.") We find that when we triangulate our data, we get invaluable information about our readers.

Triangulating is a cyclical process—analyzing, questioning, assessing, analyzing, questioning, assessing—with the teacher in control of the process. It is our questions and observations that allow us to use the information we have about our students to dig deeper and piece it together to understand what they need instructionally.

Figure 4.2
Questions That
Help to
Triangulate Data

> **What Is My Purpose?**
> *Diagnostic, formative, and summative:*
> - Do we need a diagnostic, formative, or summative tool?
> - When are we giving the assessment and how will we use the information?
> - Are we trying to assess our readers before, during, or after a period of instruction?
>
> **What Method Should I Use?**
> *Formal and informal:*
> - Do we need a formal or informal tool?
> - How are we administering the assessment, and how can we use the information?
> - Do we want to be able to compare our readers with a standard score or do we need an in-depth description of how a reader is performing daily?
>
> **What Type of Data Do I Need?**
> *Quantitative and qualitative:*
> - Do we need a quantitative or qualitative tool?
> - What kind of information are we collecting, and how can we use it?
> - Are we assessing a student's instructional level, or do we need information on the quality of that student's strategy use?

Voices from the Classroom

Triangulating Assessments

I just finished administering Mary's Developmental Reading Assessment (DRA). She read a Level 20 on the DRA with 98 percent accuracy and with some comprehension. Several questions were in my mind as I analyzed her DRA:

- Why does she have such a high accuracy rate but read with very little intonation?
- When Mary came to an unfamiliar word, she appeared to process in her head for several seconds and then read the word correctly. What strategies is she using when she is stopping? Can I teach her more efficient strategies?
- Why is Mary reading so slowly and why is she having difficulty comprehending? Is her comprehension weak because she is slowing down to figure out unfamiliar words, or is she slowing down because she is unable to grasp the information in the text?
- How well does Mary know her phonetic skills?

I dig deeper to answer my questions by administering an additional assessment in a specific area of reading: isolated phonics skills. I use the Lexia Quick Reading Test. The results show that Mary needs additional instruction in long vowels, vowel combinations, multisyllabic words, and high-frequency words. On many portions of the assessment Mary answered the items correctly but did not pass the section because she was responding very slowly. When I triangulate my data by comparing the results of the isolated phonics assessment with the DRA results, I find that in both cases Mary had difficulty solving words efficiently and did not commit words to memory once she solved them. This gives me a better understanding of what is slowing down Mary's reading progress.

I decide to focus my instruction on strategies to commit high-frequency words to memory, to use the rules for long vowels when decoding unknown words, and to decode multisyllabic words. I will focus my conferring notes during instruction on how she is using the strategies I am teaching her to decode with more automaticity. I want to notice if these strategies help her decode more effectively and efficiently. If they do and her fluency improves, I then want to assess her comprehension again to see if it is affected. I ultimately want to know if the weakness in comprehension is linked to her lack of fluency and automaticity in decoding or if it is an unrelated issue. ◀

Although the cyclical nature of triangulating—analyzing, questioning, and assessing—may put teachers in control of the process, they do not have control over all the assessments we use with our students. Our common assessments are often mandated. Although they may not be the tools we would choose, they do give us an opportunity to triangulate our data by providing a source of information to use alongside the assessments we do choose. Common assessments allow us to draw on different types of assessments and assessments taken at different intervals, and to look for both patterns and inconsistencies across assessments (Boudett, City, and Murnane 2005). Common assessments are given to all students at a certain grade level, so they provide an opportunity to compare results within a classroom, grade level, school, district, or nation.

Common assessments give us a starting point in the process—we analyze these data and ask questions about our students. These initial questions help us set up authentic learning experiences in our classroom to observe students' actions and note their responses. In this case the process begins by analyzing a formal piece of data and then triangulating it with more formative, informal data. At times, however,

Figure 4.3
Drowning in
Data

the process begins when we notice something surprising in our classroom data and then want to triangulate our observation with a more formal or diagnostic assessment. We have even found ourselves triangulating with more than one piece of formal data. For example, a student may not perform well on a state standards-based test and we are surprised. We then follow up that assessment with a formal, norm-referenced assessment like the GRADE or the Stanford 10 to see how the student performs against peers on this type of an assessment.

The problem we find with this process is that when we triangulate our data by using multiple sources, formal and informal, we end up with piles of paper to analyze (Figure 4.3).

We have all seen our desk look like this, and although the picture is funny, we recognize that this is no way to find the stories of our students. Whether we are looking at our class data or several pieces of data on one student, we cannot organize ourselves to plan and understand readers when we are buried in paper. When we find ourselves in this situation, we use displays to find our way out from under the piles.

The Power of Displays

Displays are pictures or graphs that highlight the patterns or inconsistencies in data. When we take the piles of paper and create one or two pictures from it, it is amazing how quickly our attention is directed and we can find the story. Let's take a look at Zachary's drawing again

(Figure 4.1). Ms. Frasier created a display when she chose to place the two portraits side by side. If she hadn't analyzed the portraits side by side, she might not have asked the same questions. The display directed her attention to the difference in quality between the two portraits and pushed her to find additional sources of data to answer her questions.

When we make a display, we think about our purpose in assessing, the type of information the assessment tool we are using provides, and what information we need about our readers. Then we think about the type of display that will help us organize the data so that we can analyze it easily and notice patterns and inconsistencies. We try to focus on only one aspect of the data at a time and triangulate that one aspect with either multiple sources or intervals, such as one question type, one standard, one group of students, one student, one thing that surprised us in the data, and so on, so that we are not overwhelmed by trying to analyze too many aspects at one time.

We use many different types of displays to help us organize and analyze our assessment data. The most powerful part of a display is the process of thinking through how you will create it; creating the display is really part of triangulating the data. Once we do an initial analysis, we ask more questions, gather additional sources of data, and then make a display that will help us triangulate. The display compares more than one piece of data by showing the multiple pieces of information side by side. When we make the display, we think about how we want to analyze multiple sources of data and the picture we create helps us draw conclusions. The best displays immediately cause us to ask questions—as with Zachary's self-portraits. These questions further push us into the act of assessing.

Using Displays to Triangulate Data

The following section provides some examples of displays and how they can be used to triangulate multiple sources of data. First we describe each display and then we give an example of how we might use it to triangulate the information to either inform instruction or signal the need to collect additional data.

Bar Graphs

Bar graphs are powerful displays for looking at data in different categories. Data can be categorized by month, year, question type, skill, or

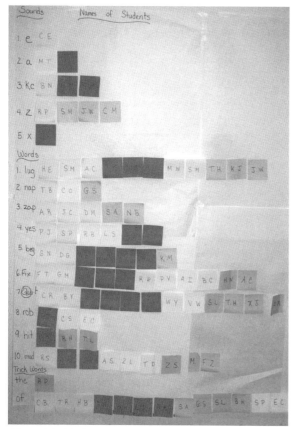

Figure 4.4 Horizontal Bar Graph

age group. Typically the categories appear along the horizontal axis and the height of the bar shows the value of each category. Bar graphs are helpful when you are looking at the same information over many years or months or when you want to get a picture of how a group of students are doing with several skills.

The graph in Figure 4.4 is a horizontal bar graph. This group of teachers used the results of several phonics assessments to identify which students in their grade level needed additional instruction on specific phonics skills. To make this bar graph, each teacher had a different color of sticky note and wrote his or her students' initials on the notes. Then the teachers placed the sticky notes on the graph. The graph helped the teachers plan upcoming small-group and whole-class lessons for their entire grade level.

Stem-and-Leaf Graphs

A stem-and-leaf graph is simply a frequency distribution graph. A frequency distribution is a tool for organizing data. We use it to group data into categories and show the number of observations in each category. The stem part of the graph is the left-hand column, which displays the category of scores, and the right-hand columns are the leaf part, which lists the observations.

Figure 4.5 is a stem-and-leaf graph of the DIBELS results for Stephanie's entire kindergarten class. Notice how the results of all three DIBELS assessments are shown in this one display. The left-hand column displays the score and the right-hand columns show how each student in the class performed on each assessment. This graph also shows when a student is meeting the benchmark on each assessment by using a different color to indicate the cut score. The shaded areas show which students did not meet the winter benchmarks.

Figure 4.5 Stem-and-Leaf Graph

Score	Letter Naming Fluency	Phoneme Segmentation	Nonsense Word Fluency
WINTER DIBELS—KINDERGARTEN—INSTRUCTIONAL GROUPING			
50+			
50			
49	Karen, Matthew		
48	Sophia		
47			
45,46		Sophia, Caroline	
43,44		Matthew	
42			
41		Eric	
40			
39	Abigail, Rachael	Isaac	Sophia
37,38	Eric	Abigail, George	
35,36	George	Cally, Julie	
33,34	Timothy, Luca	Karen, Samantha	
31,32	Erica	Rachael	Eric
30,			
29			
28			
27	Christina, Samantha		
25,26	Caroline, Julie		Karen, Matthew
24	Cally, Aidan, Mark	Timothy	
21,22,23		Luca, Erica	Timothy, Luca, Erica
20			Samantha
19			
17,18	Isaac		Christina, Cally, Julie, Rachael
16			
15			Caroline
14		Christina	Abigail
13			
11,12			George, Aidan, Isaac
10			
9			
8			
7		Aidan	
6			Mark
5		Mark	
4			
3			
2			
1			
0			

↑ Stem   ↑ Leaf   ↑   ↑

☐ Low Risk   ☐ Some Risk   ■ At-Risk

Since the DIBELS is a universal screener and does not diagnose exactly what students need to learn, Stephanie plans to collect additional assessment information on the students who did not meet the benchmarks. She asks the following questions to help her choose which assessments to administer:

- Do I need a diagnostic, formative, or summative tool for gathering more information on the students who scored below benchmark?
- Do I need a formal or informal tool?
- Do I need a quantitative or qualitative tool?

Refer to page 66 for information about which assessments Stephanie chooses to help her triangulate the data.

Data Walls

Data walls are displays that share relevant data with the entire school faculty. They can be displayed as graphs, tables, or texts, depending on the type of information collected. Since data walls are visible to so many people, the display can encourage collaboration to support at-risk readers, highlight achievements, and increase everyone's assessment literacy.

Figure 4.6a shows the entire school's reading-data results by grade level. Each student is represented by one sticky note that includes an identifying student number. Grade-level teams analyze multiple pieces

Figure 4.6a
Data Wall

of assessment data to determine which students are meeting or exceeding grade-level benchmarks, which students are inconsistently meeting grade-level benchmarks, and which students are reading well below benchmark. Each student's sticky note is placed in the appropriate spot on the data wall to represent his or her category of progress. The three background colors on the data wall represent the categories of student progress. The top row, which is green, represents "meeting or exceeding benchmark." The middle row, which is yellow, represents "inconsistently meeting benchmark." And the bottom row, which is red, represents "not meeting benchmark."

After each student's sticky note has been placed on the board (Figure 4.6b), teachers put a corresponding colored dot to match the color of the category on it (for example, a green dot means the green category, or "meeting or exceeding benchmark"). At future meetings, students who are being moved between the categories receive another colored dot sticker indicating their new category of student progress. Notice how some students have several colored dots on their sticky note. This shows their movement between the different categories. The display makes it easy to see quickly which students have grown and which have not. Notice on the data wall in Figure 4.6b that the teachers placed a star on the students' sticky notes if they received a proficient score on the state exam.

Figure 4.6b
Close-up of Data Wall

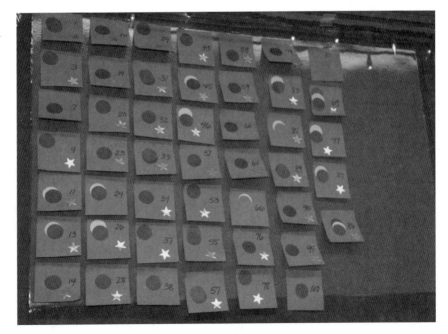

As we look at this display, many questions arise:

- Who are the students reading below benchmark?
- Who are the students who have not made progress?
- Who are the students who passed the state test but are categorized in yellow or red?
- Why are they scoring below benchmark on classroom assessments but passing the state test?

Since we can't delve more deeply into all the issues, we decide to focus on the students who scored well on the state test but poorly on their classroom assessments. These students' scores are puzzling, and we want to understand why they are scoring inconsistently. We decide to triangulate the data for these students by analyzing their

- DRA2,
- phonics unit test,
- teacher conferring notes, and
- student reading notebook responses.

When we look at all of these side by side, we get a clearer picture of the strengths and weaknesses of these readers. A few of them seem to be doing minimal work during reading workshop. These students have very few entries in their reading notebooks and appear distracted during reading workshop. Our conference notes document that they have difficulty choosing books, abandon books frequently, and are often not engaged in reading. When we look at other assessment data, we notice that these students scored well on the DRA2 and the phonics unit test. Why are they in intervention? We clearly need to engage these readers. We decide we need to further triangulate these data by talking with these students, sharing their data with each of them, and getting their thoughts about it.

One student who scored well on the state exam but is in intervention appears to have different needs. When we triangulate his data, it is clear that he has difficulty decoding multisyllabic words. Although the state testing data do not reveal this weakness, his problems are highlighted on the phonics unit test, the DRA2, and in our conference notes. Why was this student able to read the passages on the state test? Was it the length of the passages, the vocabulary used in the passages, or did the multiple choice questions make it easier for him? On the

DRA2 the student tried to decode unfamiliar words when he was reading aloud, but it was clear that he could not do it. We decide to assess this student's decoding skills so we can identify exactly which skills he needs to learn.

Line Graphs

Line graphs are displays that show how one data point changes over time. One axis of the graph shows the assessment scale, and the other shows the length of time. Line graphs are helpful displays when we want to look at data for one student or a group of students over an extended period of time.

The line graph in Figure 4.7 measures how long a book group engaged in meaningful discussion. The students in this book group noticed they were getting into dead-end conversations. Their group goals were to choose better questions to discuss and to use conversational techniques to build on one another's thoughts rather than taking the conversation off-track. They used this display to help them measure whether the strategies they tried were helping to increase the length of their discussions.

Figure 4.7
Line Graph:
Building Stamina
for Book Club
Discussions

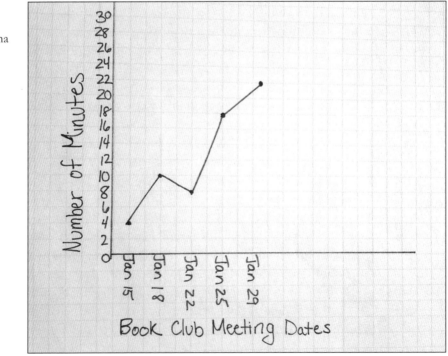

Once the students noticed their stamina increasing, they wanted to focus on the quality of their conversations as well. They decided to measure how often they referenced the text, how often they referred to one another's thinking, and how often their thinking changed or grew as a result of the book group discussion.

Conferring Notes

At first, we did not think of conferring notes (Figure 4.8a) as a display. We took notes to document our thoughts, observations, and questions about readers for years without really using them to triangulate and teach. We now design our conferring notes so that important information stands out and patterns are displayed, helping us quickly analyze what is happening for our readers.

Figure 4.8a Conferring Notes with Learning Goals

Date/Title	Observation and Instruction Notes
1/17 *Zack Files 1*	Not sure how to read the dialogue. Isn't sure who is speaking. Rereading to figure it out.
1/22 *Zack Files 2*	Reading dialogue a bit better but not stopping at the punctuation. Needs to picture who is talking to keep track of characters
1/25 *Time for Kids*	Skimming the articles. Not sure he is really reading any of them. Reviewed how to choose an article and read to learn new information.

In these conferring notes, the teacher simply highlights the student's learning goals so that they stand out on the page.

As we look over the conferring notes in Figure 4.8b, some questions come to mind:

- Why is Joanie reading so slowly? Is it because she is writing too frequently, or is something else going on?
- Is she reading accurately?
- Is she comprehending?
- Is she enjoying this book?

Figure 4.8b Conferring Notes for Joanie

Student Name: Joanie

Goals:
- Read for longer amounts of time
- Infer character traits and motivations
- Take notes while reading

> When the goals are written on top, it is easy for the teacher to see what Joanie is working on. The column below displays the progress she is making on a particular goal.

Date/Title	Observation and Instruction Notes	Instructional Goals: Next Steps to Meet Goals
10/5 *Stone Fox*	• Can summarize chapter • Can identify what the character says and does but needs to learn to infer traits	• Infer character traits
10/8 *Stone Fox*	• Recorded character traits of Willie • Is she reading enough pages?	• Needs to find the most appropriate evidence to support her inference • Notice how much she is reading
10/11 *Stone Fox*	• Still hasn't finished book. Watched her while reading and noticed that she is writing several sentences every few minutes.	• Teach her when to take notes and how to take notes

Engagement   Text   Metacognition   Reader Response

> This column highlights how long Joanie has been reading *Stone Fox*. Since Joanie has forty-five minutes for independent reading each day, we know that she should have been able to finish *Stone Fox* in just a few days.

In order to triangulate our conferring notes on Joanie, we will take a running record of her reading a few pages of *Stone Fox* to assess her accuracy. We will also ask talk with Joanie to assess her comprehension and to see how she is enjoying the book. After that, we will look through her notebook to see what she has been writing. These steps will help us pinpoint her next learning goals and areas to assess.

Messy Sheets

The Messy Sheet (Figure 4.9) is a display we created with Judy Hardy, a teacher in Wayland, Massachusetts, to help us see patterns as we tri-

Figure 4.9
Messy Sheet

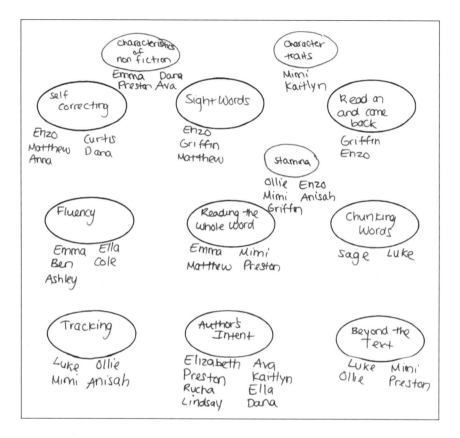

angulate our data. When we are analyzing several pieces of data side by side, we take note of any key concepts that need to be taught. We write the key concept in a circle and the names of the students who would benefit from this instruction underneath. This display helps us transform piles of data into a one-page plan that organizes our instruction. The Messy Sheet in Figure 4.9 was created as we triangulated our conferring notes, reading notebooks, and the Fountas and Pinnell Benchmark Assessment System. We documented patterns we noticed across the three types of assessment on the Messy Sheet. When we look at this display, it helps us see the small groups we need to teach. For example, Mimi and Kaitlyn need instruction on inferring character traits while reading.

Picture Graphs

The display in Figure 4.10 is a picture graph. We use it to help us think about our teaching priorities. As we analyze our assessment data, we

Figure 4.10 Picture Graph

What Do the Students Know?	What Do the Students Need to Learn?
Books they love Authors Stamina Structure and routine of reading workshop Decoding strategies Monitoring for meaning Fluency	Structure of retelling✓✓✓✓✓✓✓✓✓ Setting✓✓✓✓✓✓✓✓✓ Skip and reread✓✓✓✓✓✓✓ Monitor as you read Focus during reading✓✓✓✓✓✓✓✓✓✓✓ Fluency✓✓✓✓✓✓✓✓✓✓

ask ourselves what our students know and what they need to learn, and then we record our observations on this graph. Each time we find another student who needs to learn a concept we have already listed, we put a check mark next to it. Once the display is finished, we can quickly see which concepts most students have mastered and which concepts most need to learn.

This graph may also help us decide to get some additional data on the students. For example, based on the data in the picture graph in Figure 4.10, we choose to get additional data on the students' engagement during reading workshop by observing them and taking notes during the upcoming week. We also plan some small-group sessions to talk with the students about why they are having difficulty focusing when reading independently.

The CAFE Menu

We use the CAFE Menu (Figure 4.11), from "The Sisters," as an interactive display. It allows us to triangulate our data and then set instructional goals with students. We love how we can quickly look at this display and determine which strategies the class is working on and which strategies individual students are working on. We can see our small groups emerge and notice how our students are progressing. We also love how students play an active role in creating and analyzing this display. It is wonderful for goal setting with them.

Running Record Error Analysis

When we do the error analysis of a running record, we have made a display (Figure 4.12). This display highlights which strategies a reader tends to use when he or she comes to an unknown word.

Figure 4.11
The CAFE Menu

Figure 4.12
Running Record
Error Analysis

When we analyze an error analysis we ask these questions:

- What type of information did the student use when he or she made the mistake?
- Is there a pattern to the mistakes the student is making?
- What behaviors does the student use to problem-solve?
- Is there more information I need to collect to understand why the student is making these errors?

In the displayed error analysis we may want to teach this student how to cross-check with meaning and how to use the story and picture(s) to think about what word fits contextually.

Jump-Starting the Assessment Process

Once we are in the midst of triangulating our data and using displays, the process takes on a life of its own. Each display helps us analyze the data, ask questions, and decide how to make the next display we need. Jump-starting this process can be a bit trickier. How do you know what you want to see? What do you want to compare? What type of display will work best? What data should you use? These are all questions that come to mind for us. Our first step in beginning this process is to think about our purpose for assessing and the type of information our assessment tools provide (Figure 4.2). We think about what type of data we have and what it can and cannot tell us. This helps us think about the kind of questions we can expect to answer with the data.

Some good times to jump-start the triangulating process are when we have some common data, when we have just finished assessing our class in an assessment cycle, or when we have a reader who is puzzling us. We typically have common data on our readers three times a year—beginning, midyear, and end of year—and individual data more often for our readers at-risk. When we finish assessing, we often are left with piles of paper that we need to sort through and analyze. Some of our common assessments give us a display to begin the process—our state test and any norm-referenced test typically provide displays for analysis. Other assessments, such as the DRA, the DIBELS, or the Fountas and Pinnell Benchmark Assessment System, do not come with a display unless you use the software to create one. When we are beginning the process and have multiple assessment tools to triangulate on our class or on one student, here are some questions we think about and some displays we find helpful:

What Do I Need to Teach?

- We use picture graphs (Figure 4.10) as we look at the different assessments to capture areas of instruction for our students.
- We use the Messy Sheet (Figure 4.9) as we look at the different assessments to capture which students need instruction in different areas. This helps us plan our small-group lessons.
- We use the CAFE Menu (Figure 4.11) to help us organize small-group, whole-class, and individual lessons.

Who Are My Students of Concern?

- We use a data wall (Figure 4.6) to compare students. This helps us quickly highlight those who are at-risk. Once we identify the students who did not make benchmark, we typically look more closely at their assessments and triangulate by collecting more data on them.
- We use a stem-and-leaf graph (Figure 4.5) when we want to compare students across more than one assessment measure. This gives us a full profile of how each student is doing and allows us to identify groups of students who need support. It also helps us see some inconsistencies and patterns.

Which of My Students Are Scoring Above Benchmark?

- We use a stem-and-leaf graph (Figure 4.5) and a data wall (Figure 4.6) to compare students with benchmarks. This helps us quickly see which students are below benchmark. Once we identify them, we typically look more closely at their assessments and triangulate by collecting more data to determine the next steps of instruction.

Who Do I Need Additional Information About?

- We use the stem-and-leaf graph (Figure 4.5) and the data wall (Figure 4.6) to highlight surprises or inconsistencies. Both these displays allow us to compare students with benchmarks and with each other. When we do this, we often notice things we did not expect or things that concern us. This pushes us to gather more data, triangulate, and continue to look for information to find the story of these readers.

Voices from the Classroom

Creating Displays

Tammy and Stephanie use a stem-and-leaf graph to learn more about Stephanie's kindergartners.

"I'm done!" Stephanie smiles as she relishes finishing her winter assessments. Assessing eighteen kindergartners is no small feat. This year, instead of just recording each student's scores on the front of the booklet and turning them in, Stephanie asked Tammy to help her find a more effective way of analyzing how her students are doing. Tammy shared a stem-and-leaf display and explained how this display can help organize all the information about Stephanie's eighteen students on one piece of paper (Figure 4.5).

"With a stem-and-leaf display, we can look at all your students across several assessment tools so you can compare one student across multiple tools and compare students with each other," Tammy said. "This display makes it easy to identify students of concern. See—Aidan and Mark jump out first. They are both scoring at-risk on this screener. We might want to spend some additional time with them over the next few weeks. These assessments are universal screeners, so they will not help you diagnose exactly what these students need to learn. We will need to dig more deeply and triangulate these data with a diagnostic and qualitative assessment tool that will give you some in-depth information about what these at-risk readers already know and what they need to learn next."

After talking through the display, Stephanie came up with this action plan:

1. **Letter Naming Fluency:** Six students did not do well in Letter Naming Fluency. I will compare the results of this assessment with the Letter ID assessment of Marie Clay's (which is formative, quantitative, and qualitative) that I gave in December. Since the DIBELS is a timed assessment, I wonder whether these students know the names of their letters when they are not being timed. I will also set up a letter-sorting activity next week and watch and assess as these students work with the letter tiles.

2. **Phoneme Segmentation:** Doing poorly on the Phoneme Segmentation task in February of kindergarten is worrisome to me. Since three students did not meet the benchmark, I will triangulate these data by giving them a diagnostic, qualitative phonemic awareness assessment. I need to understand exactly what aspects of

phonemic awareness these students know and what aspects they need to learn. [Refer to Chapter 3 for a list of possible assessments for this area of reading.]

3. **Nonsense Word Fluency:** Four readers did not meet the benchmark for Nonsense Word Fluency. When I look at the stem-and-leaf display, I see that Mark, Aidan, and Isaac did not meet the benchmark for identifying letters and sounds on the other assessment tools, so it makes sense that they would not meet this benchmark yet. George is a bit more puzzling. When I look at the stem-and-leaf display, I notice he did fine in Letter Naming Fluency and Phoneme Segmentation but missed the Nonsense Word Fluency benchmark. Why did he score so poorly? I will take a closer look at his DIBELS booklet to see why he scored poorly and then meet with him one-on-one to watch him blend words. Maybe observing him doing this will give me more insight.

By taking the time to make a display, Stephanie was able to come up with a plan to triangulate by gathering more data to inform her instruction. This display has identified the students about whom she needs to gather more diagnostic information to understand their needs as readers. ◀

Jennifer Allen, in *Becoming a Literacy Leader*, reminds us that

the purpose of administering a reading assessment to students is not simply to calculate reading levels, but rather to analyze the assessment to learn more about students' reading behaviors. It is our responsibility as educators to take the time to analyze and interpret the assessments we give our students so that we can find out how we can tailor our instruction to meet their needs. (2006, 130)

Triangulating our data and using displays not only makes analysis more efficient but also helps us put into practice what we know for sure so we move beyond the numbers and focus on instruction.

THE STORIES WE CARRY

Using a Display to Triangulate Data on a Student

Jacob was an at-risk reader entering the fourth grade. To learn more about him as a reader, we decided to take a look at the data that had been collected on him during the previous few years. We made the line graph in Figure S4.1 to show Jacob's fluency rate over a three-year period.

Figure S4.1
Fluency
Monitoring
Over Time:
Jacob

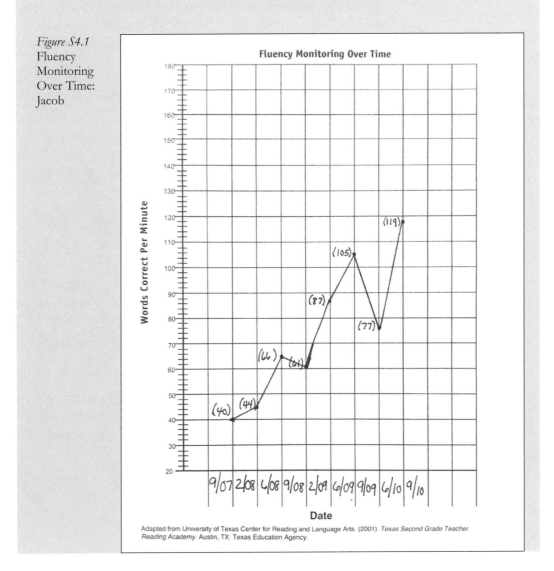

Adapted from University of Texas Center for Reading and Language Arts. (2001). *Texas Second Grade Teacher Reading Academy*. Austin, TX: Texas Education Agency.

Line graphs are displays that show how one data point changes over time. One axis of the graph shows the assessment scale, and the other shows the length of time. The display triangulates the data because it shows data over time, at different intervals. Looking at this one aspect of our common assessment on Jacob raised many questions for us:

- How much was Jacob reading both at home and at school?
- What did he like to read?
- Was Jacob's reading rate affecting his comprehension?
- Was he reading accurately with appropriate phrasing and expression, or was his reading choppy and/or monotone?
- Why did his rate slip so much over the summer?

To answer these questions, we decided to triangulate these data and collect additional data from multiple sources so that we could understand what was happening for Jacob as a reader. We looked over Jacob's book logs (informal data) from the first few weeks of school to see what he was reading and administered a reading interview survey (informal data). Through these data we learned that although Jacob liked books that were suspenseful or funny he could not name any authors he enjoyed reading. From his book log, we learned that he was reading only five to ten pages each day at reading workshop. New questions emerged:

- Why was he reading only five to ten pages?
- Was he matched well with texts?
- How was his comprehension?

To answer these questions we wanted more data, so we administered the Developmental Reading Assessment 2 (DRA2) to get a more systematic observation of the strategies he used as a reader and a more quantitative look at his accuracy, fluency, and comprehension. This assessment gave us additional information to understand Jacob as a reader. Jacob read slowly, but with accuracy and good comprehension. We decided that his repeated regression in reading rate might be less of a speed issue and more about engagement and interest. This would explain why his rate increased during each school year, when he at least read some during the school day, and then plummeted during the summer. When we triangulated the reading rate data display with other pieces of assessment data, it helped us piece together the story of Jacob as a reader and identify his next instructional steps. We decided to teach him strategies for building his reading stamina and engaging in text by joining some reading partnerships to discuss the books he was reading. We wanted to continue to assess his engagement in reading by talking with him about his books, monitoring his book log, and assessing his comprehension to make certain he understood the characters and themes in his books.

CHAPTER 5

Assessing Authentically, Every Day

I have worked hard to reclaim my original concept of assessment and remember why I valued it in the first place. Teachers have power over formative assessments—the assessments that matter most to learning. When formative assessments are given along the way, they help teachers know what students need and also give students ideas on how to improve. They feed teachers and, more important, feed students so they can grow.

—Cris Tovani, *So What Do They Really Know?* (2011)

▶ Our class is studying theme and how readers infer themes throughout a text to determine the author's purpose or message. We are teaching this concept in our interactive read-aloud and in our small-group sessions. Students are tracking themes in their notebooks and citing evidence to support their ideas. As we analyze our students' notebooks, we notice that they seem to be confused about the concept of theme and how to determine the themes of a text. Many of the students are retelling what happens in the text but aren't really focusing on theme. We decide to design a lesson that will give us some insight into why the students are struggling with this concept. We begin the lesson by sharing with the students what we are noticing about their understanding of theme. We ask them to turn and talk with a partner about theme and how they determine possible themes of a text. We listen in on the partner discussions and take notes on what we are hearing. We realize that many students are confusing the concepts of plot and theme. We pull the group back together and ask them to share their discussions. Ella shares what she discussed with her partner: "Theme is what happens in the story—you know, the big problem. We use prediction to help us figure out the theme or what is going to happen." We do not want the students to be further confused, so we stop the sharing and begin an explicit lesson on the difference between plot and theme. ◀

Assessment cannot be separated from instruction. It is not an "add-on"; it is what we do every day as teachers. The cyclical process of triangulating—analyzing, questioning, and assessing—is embedded in instruction. It is simply how we teach. Some call it the "teachable moment"—the moment when a student says something that causes us to veer from our original teaching plan. What we hear or see from our students causes us to pause, observe, assess, analyze, and adjust our instruction. Experiencing these teachable moments and seeing learning "click" for our readers is magical. That magic is why we teach, and assessment is an essential part of it.

The pedagogical beliefs that we "know to be true" define our understanding of the importance of assessing in the moment to inform our instructional decisions (see Chapter 2). These beliefs also tell us why it is essential that we use this information alongside formal data. We believe this pedagogy needs to be included in the bigger context of assessment in our profession:

- Piaget's work taught us to create learning experiences so we can observe the behaviors of our students as they are learning. When we see how our students construct knowledge, we have a better understanding of how they learn.
- Vygotsky's work showed us the importance of viewing *assessment* as not only what students can do well, but also what students need to learn. When we notice and analyze what our students do when they encounter difficulty in learning, it gives us a window into what they need to learn next.
- Peter Johnston's work reminds us "that the most educationally significant assessment takes place in classrooms, moment to moment, among teachers and students" (1997, 7).
- Carol Ann Tomlinson's research on differentiated instruction and the role assessment plays in meeting a wide range of learners' needs is critical to why we assess in the moment.
- Pearson and Gallagher's instructional framework within the gradual release of responsibility model provides opportunities to observe which skills and strategies students use when faced with a challenge and then use those observations to plan next steps in instruction.

It is Marie Clay's work, however, that serves as our constant reminder of why we cannot lose sight of the critical need to assess as we teach:

Effective teaching calls for a third kind of assessment designed to record how the child works on tasks and to inform teaching as it occurs. Classroom teachers can observe students as they construct responses by moving among them while they work.

They can observe how individuals change over time by keeping good records. And they can allow children to take different learning paths to the same outcomes because they are clearly aware of the learning that is occurring. (Clay 1993, 4)

When we include our classroom data in the definition of assessment, we avoid the risk of making decisions based on one number. In this type of assessment, we are observing our students as they are learning, and instruction is embedded in the process of triangulating. We collect formative, informal, and qualitative data as we are teaching. Most of these data falls into two categories: observations or student work. Here are some examples of what we collect:

Observations
conference notes
small-group notes
turn-and-talk notes
engagement notes
reading behavior notes—running records, inventories, time
    samplings, etc.

Student Work
notebook entries
logs
surveys
reflections
informal tests/quizzes
constructed responses
projects

Now, theory gets us only so far in an elementary classroom. How do we put all our beliefs into practice? When we think about creating a community of readers—readers who are strategic, meta-cognitive, and independent—systems and structures are what come to mind. How can we set up a classroom culture that supports our need to observe and assess? How do we structure our schedule and design an environment to support the creation of learning experiences that give us opportunities to watch our readers in the process of learning? What types of note taking will be easy enough for us to follow through and do? How should we organize our notes so that we can find them and use them?

Structures

Structures are how we organize the time and space in our classroom to support assessing as we teach. We use a workshop model because it provides a structure in which students can work independently or with partners so we have time to assess and teach smaller groups. The workshop model reflects the gradual release of responsibility model of instruction and gives us time to watch our students as they learn in whole-class, small-group, and individual lessons. We believe it is essential to have each type of setting to observe and assess our readers because it helps us understand how they are transferring the strategies we are teaching them as they read.

Time is a precious resource in our classroom, and we never seem to have enough of it. The pressure to "fit it all in" sometimes causes us to lose sight of the importance of just hanging back and watching. Kathy Collins says in *Growing Readers*, "I like to watch and note how children approach and work on the same text. The way that children approach the book is important information to note because it tells us something about what they already know and think about reading" (2004, 94). We completely agree that we should do this, but we have to admit that there are times when we feel the pressure of time and jump right into teaching. We use a lesson structure that includes time to question and observe during the lesson. This has helped us have an assessment stance as we teach.

Lucy Calkins (2001) gave us the framework we needed to structure our lessons to include time to assess. In her framework of a conference—research, decide, teach—assessment and instruction are happening simultaneously and build off one another continually. To effectively use our instructional time with students as an opportunity to assess, we always keep that framework—research, decide, teach—in mind whether we are working with one student, a small group, or the whole class.

Our lesson structure (Figure 5.1) is designed to begin with a question or observation. We begin our lessons (whole-class, small-group or one-on-one) with an assessment stance by asking formative questions or observing to get an understanding of where students are in the learning process:

What are you working on right now in _____?
How's it going with _____?

What have you been doing lately as a reader with _____?
What have you learned about _____?
How does learning about _____ help you as a reader?
Where are the tricky parts?
Show me (or your partner) where _____.
Explain to your partner how you _____.
Talk about how you figured out _____.

Figure 5.1
Lesson Planning
Form

We jot the questions we want to ask or the behaviors we want to observe before the lesson begins in the Pre-assessment box so that we remember to collect these data before we begin teaching.

Here we record possible questions to ask students during conferences. Listing a few possible questions or prompts ahead of time helps us focus the data we collect on the learning goal we are teaching.

Anchor Lesson:		
Pre-assessment		**Notes to Build Next Lesson**
Select the materials.		
Name the strategy. Explain. *"I have noticed that . . ."* *"A strategy readers use is . . ."*		
Demonstrate the strategy. Say: *Think aloud.* **Show:** *Model.* **Explain:** *How this will help them as a reader.*		
Provide guided practice. Invite the students to practice the strategy with teacher guidance.		
Provide independent practice. Remind students before they go off to reading workshop.		
Conference Points		
Share/Reinforce		

We collect assessment data during guided and independent practice. This is a time when we can gather important formative data. Asking questions helps us pinpoint specific places of confusion and makes our teaching points more precise. We also use turn-and-talk as a method to listen in on students' conversations and gather data.

We also take notes during the group share as students tell us what they learned about themselves as readers at the end of reading workshop. As students share, we listen in to find future teaching points for upcoming lessons.

These questions are typically linked to the instructional goals we have identified so that we can pre-assess how students are progressing with the content we are teaching. We need to know our goals and the essential concepts within those goals in order to know how we are assessing our students. Asking questions around the objectives we are teaching provides immediate feedback on what students know and what they need to learn next. It gives us the information we need so we can be more precise in our teaching.

Systems to Record Our Observations and Student Work

We want to use the ongoing, informal, formative assessments we collect to dig deeper and triangulate the more formal data we have about our readers. We find this difficult to do if we do not collect and organize our classroom data in a systematic way. We try to record what we are noticing systematically so we can use the information diagnostically in the process of triangulating—analyzing, questioning, assessing. When we are teaching, we take the time to document what we notice about the students in the moment so that we can use the information right away to focus our instruction.

Recording Our Observations

Following are some forms we use to help us take notes systematically.

Conferring Notes

What is most important about taking conferring notes is that they help us remember the teaching priorities for each student. Once we ask questions and watch a student in the process of learning, we analyze what we have observed and decide on instructional goals. The data we gather and the decisions we make need to be documented so we can use them to plan future whole-class, small-group, and individual lessons. We find it helpful when our conferring form has a place to record both our general observations and specific learning goals. We like to have boxes for both, because after we take notes, we take a moment to think about the next teaching priority for each student. Does the student need to continue working on his or her current goal or is he or she ready to move on to a new teaching priority? When the form highlights the goals, it helps us quickly find the information we need when we are using our conferring notes to triangulate with other sources of data. Figures 4.8a and b are samples of completed conferring forms. A blank individual conferring form is available in the appendix.

Reading Behavior Notes

We use running records to systematically observe the skills and strategies our readers are using. (See Figure 3.3 for a sample.) Clay's running record is one of the observation surveys she designed to help teachers systematically observe students in the process of learning. Clay's book *An Observation Survey* (1993) focuses on several different types of assessments teachers can use with their students as they teach.

We use Clay's theory of systematically observing reading behaviors to design other types of inventories that focus on the specific behaviors we need to assess. Figure 5.2 is an example of a strategy inventory that we designed specifically for one student. We use this inventory to create a picture graph of the strategies we observe a reader actively using. Each time the reader uses the strategy, we note it on the picture graph.

Figure 5.2
Strategy
Inventory

Name: Hannah
Date: May 25
Book: *Five Silly Fishermen*
Level: G

Strategy Inventory

Read the picture	++
Chunk it	++++
Tap it out	+++++++
Skip it—What makes sense?	
Flip the vowel	++
Self-correct	++
Monitor—comments/flipping/laughing	+
Other	

This display works nicely because a student and a teacher can analyze the data together. A student can easily read the check marks and see which strategies he or she is using frequently and which ones he or she needs to use more regularly. We can see from the example in Figure 5.2 that this child relies on phonics to figure out unfamiliar words. In upcoming lessons we will teach her how to cross-check (use her phonics and the meaning of the text to solve unfamiliar words). Because we have only one check mark in the monitoring box, we will need to teach her to think about the text as she is reading. Here is what we might write in her conferring notes based on this picture graph:

Date/Title	Observation and Instruction Notes	Instructional Goals: Next Steps to Meet Goals
5/25 *Five Silly Fisherman*	• Tapping out—first strategy used • If tapping doesn't work, she looks for parts. • Not laughing	• Skip it—What makes sense?

Small Group

We use the form in Figure 5.3 to document our goals for our small groups and the students' progression toward those goals. We want to make certain that our students have time to truly explore, practice, and integrate the strategies they are learning with the ones they have already learned. For this to happen, we use this form to hold ourselves accountable for giving our students extended time to focus on a few goals. For most of our students, we want to focus on the same instructional goals for the month in our whole-class, small-group, and individual lessons so students can truly experience the gradual release of responsibility. The notes we take in our small groups should inform our upcoming whole-class and small-group lessons for these students. For students whose developmental needs are different from most of the students in our class, we use small-group lessons to focus on their specific needs. The instructional goals of these lessons will most likely differ from the whole-class instructional goals, so we need to carefully document and communicate the students' progress with any other teachers who are providing them with instruction. A blank small-group form is available in the appendix.

Figure 5.3 Small-Group Instruction Form for Guided Practice

Names of Students	Instructional Goals ◄	Frequency of Group ◄
Hope Jake Lucy Bill Katie	1. Read, stop, and retell so you can remember. 2. Use structure of fiction to retell (character, setting, problem, solution). We use these boxes to record the instructional goals for each small group and to jot down observational notes during small-group instruction. These notes help inform subsequent small-group meetings with these students.	2 times per week We record the number of times the group will meet during the course of a week. Notice how Jack, Chase, and Ben's group will meet daily. These students are not meeting grade-level benchmarks, so we meet with them frequently and teach them the strategies they need to learn.
Dylan Becky Jason Brad	1. Read, stop, and retell so you can remember. 2. Use structure of fiction to retell (character, setting, problem, solution).	4 times per week
Jack Chase Ben	1. Look at the picture and the first letter. 2. Think about what makes sense.	Daily
Lisa Brenda Jen Gail Bekka Sam Daniel	1. Read, stop, and retell so you can remember. 2. Use structure of nonfiction to retell (topic/detail, chronological order, etc.).	3 times per week

► Conferences

Name(s)	Instructional Goal	Name(s)	Instructional Goal
Peter/David	Just Right Books		
Hannah/Lizzy	Work Independently		

Engagement   Text   Metacognition   Reader Response

Not everyone in the class may be working in a small group during the course of a particular month. In this box we record the names of students who need specific reading conferences.

Peter and David understand retelling, but they are picking texts that are too long and difficult. We need to spend our time helping them select books that they can read easily.

Hannah and Lizzy are distracted during reading workshop. They need to learn strategies to help them stay focused on the text as they are reading. Since we are meeting with these students one-on-one or as partnerships, we record our notes on each student's individual conferring form.

Turn-and-Talk Notes

In our lesson design, we have incorporated opportunities to ask questions so that we can record our observations of what students know and what they need to learn. When we ask these questions, we often give the students a chance to turn and talk with a partner about them. When the students are talking, we listen in and write down information that will help us in the moment of that lesson and in upcoming lessons. We use the notes section on our lesson planning form (Figure 5.1) or a Messy Sheet (see Figure 4.9) to capture these notes. A blank lesson planning form and a blank Messy Sheet are available in the appendix.

Engagement Notes

When we teach, we always like to take a few seconds to hang back and watch what students are doing. We do this during independent, partner, and small-group work. We want to observe how students are engaging in their work. Are they focused? When do they get distracted? What do they do when they get distracted? How long can they remain engaged when working independently? We take notes by using the conferring notes forms of the students we are observing or a class list if we want to observe engagement from a broader perspective. Jennifer Serravallo has a wonderful inventory on assessing student engagement in her book *Teaching Reading in Small Groups*. She reminds us: "Without engagement during reading, this 'time spent reading' doesn't count. As responsible reading teachers, it is important to be vigilant when it comes to our students' engagement and to offer them strategies and techniques to help them stay motivated and engaged while reading" (2010, 20). Once we have some data, we involve the students in the analysis, the reflection, and the goal setting around any issues we are finding with engagement.

Nuts and Bolts of Housing, Taking, and Sharing Our Observational Notes

When it comes to note taking, the only thing we know for sure is that we find at least ten systems that do not work for us before we find one that does. There is no right or wrong way to organize notes. The most critical piece is that they are organized in a way that we can find them and use them to inform our instruction.

Systems for Housing Our Notes

Figure 5.4
Reading Binder

Three-Ring Binder

We sometimes use a three-ring conference binder (Figure 5.4) to house our observational notes and important pieces of student work. We have a section for each student and fill each one with the student's most recent assessment information, several blank conferring sheets, and a clear pocket sleeve for work samples. We love having all of our notes in one three-ring binder. It is transportable to and from meetings, and everything stays in one place so we can easily access and triangulate a student's information when we are analyzing data.

Figure 5.5
Hanging File
Folder Box

Hanging File Folder Box

For those of us who don't like to carry around a binder, a hanging file folder box (Figure 5.5) can be effective. The file box is set up in a corner of the classroom that is easily accessible. Each student has a hanging file, and each file contains two manila folders: Folder 1 contains the fall and spring testing data (copy of the most recent Individualized Education Plan, the actual Fountas and Pinnell Benchmark Assessment/DRA/running records, results from the Observation Survey, DIBELS data, state test results, and so on). Folder 2 contains the conferring notes for that reader.

When we want to confer, we take the folders we need. This system works well when multiple teachers are recording notes on different students simultaneously. It is also easy to use this system when working with a small group. We can take the files of the students in the small group, lay them out in front of each student, and then write notes as we work with each one individually.

Computer Spreadsheet

We have also tried converting from pencil-and-paper note taking to writing notes directly onto a laptop or iPad. In this system, we have separate file folders for each student right on the desktop or take notes in spreadsheet software, like Excel, so that they are easily accessible. We have our computers with us when we confer and pull small groups so that we can simply open a child's folder and enter our notes as we teach (see Figure 5.6).

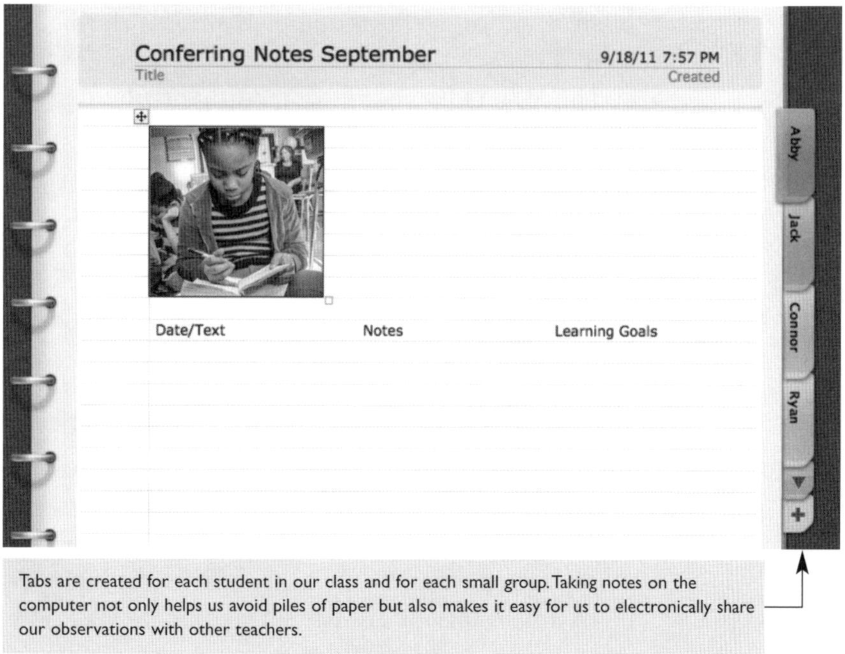
Conferring Notes September
9/18/11 7:57 PM
Title
Created
Date/Text
Notes
Learning Goals
Abby
Jack
Connor
Ryan
Tabs are created for each student in our class and for each small group. Taking notes on the computer not only helps us avoid piles of paper but also makes it easy for us to electronically share our observations with other teachers.

Figure 5.6 Electronic Conferring Notes

Housing Small-Group Notes

One struggle we continue to face is figuring out how we can use our small-group notes to plan for the group's ongoing instruction and still document the progress of its individual students. We want to have our notes readily available as we teach so we can constantly revise our instructional goals to meet our students' needs, but we also want to have notes in individual files to document what each student is doing. *And* we want this to happen without having to write the notes twice or photocopy everything. We have found that no matter which option we use, it can be difficult. Here are a few ideas we have tried:

Sticky Mailing Labels

Sometimes we prefer to take notes on individual students on mailing labels during small-group instruction. This way the notes can be easily transferred to the student's individual conferring notes and the small-group notes can remain intact.

Putting Individual Conferring Notes in Small-Group Folders

Tammy likes to put blank individual conferring notes for each student in the small-group folder. This way she can write notes on the appropriate conferring sheets for each student during the small-group lessons. The small-group notes remain together to inform instruction, and once she fills a conferring note, she files it in the student's conferring folder.

Systems for Taking Effective Notes

Taking conferring notes is a little like cooking a holiday meal for the first time. You do not know exactly what you will need, how much you will need, and what you will ultimately use. The first time Clare hosted Thanksgiving, she over-planned, over-bought, and over-provided. Now that she has done it a few times, she can pull it off and not have to eat leftovers for two weeks. When we first began taking conferring notes, it was the same way: we tried to write everything down because we did not know what we would need or how we would use the notes.

We take the time to get more efficient at taking notes. When we are given a new formal assessment to use, we take time to learn about it: what it is, what it assesses, how to administer it, and how to analyze it. We also devote time to learning how to focus our conferring notes on all areas of reading and how to document what we are noticing in a way that will allow us to use it efficiently and effectively. We use our instructional goals and student goals to help focus what we record in our notes. We take the time to reflect on our notes and determine the type of information that is most helpful to us and is essential to include.

We also use some shorthand tricks to decrease note-taking time. Clare writes in different colors for different purposes (for example, goals are always in blue ink) and uses shapes in her notes to help her identify what she needs to do: she circles things she needs to do, puts a square around goals, and draws triangles around items she needs follow-up on. Tammy uses a separate box for goals so she can quickly determine the instructional priorities for her students. These shortcuts make it easier for us to assess and record on the go. They also make it easier to find the important information we need from our notes.

Although we don't like to admit it, it is very easy to inadvertently miss meeting with one or two students when teaching over the course of a busy month. Even though we plan whom we will meet with in either small-group or individual sessions, we want to check in and make certain we have not diverted from our plan. Gail Boushey and Joan Moser use a form called the Reading/Writing Checksheet to monitor their plan (Figure 5.7). This sheet is simply a class list with

Figure 5.7
Reading/Writing
Checksheet

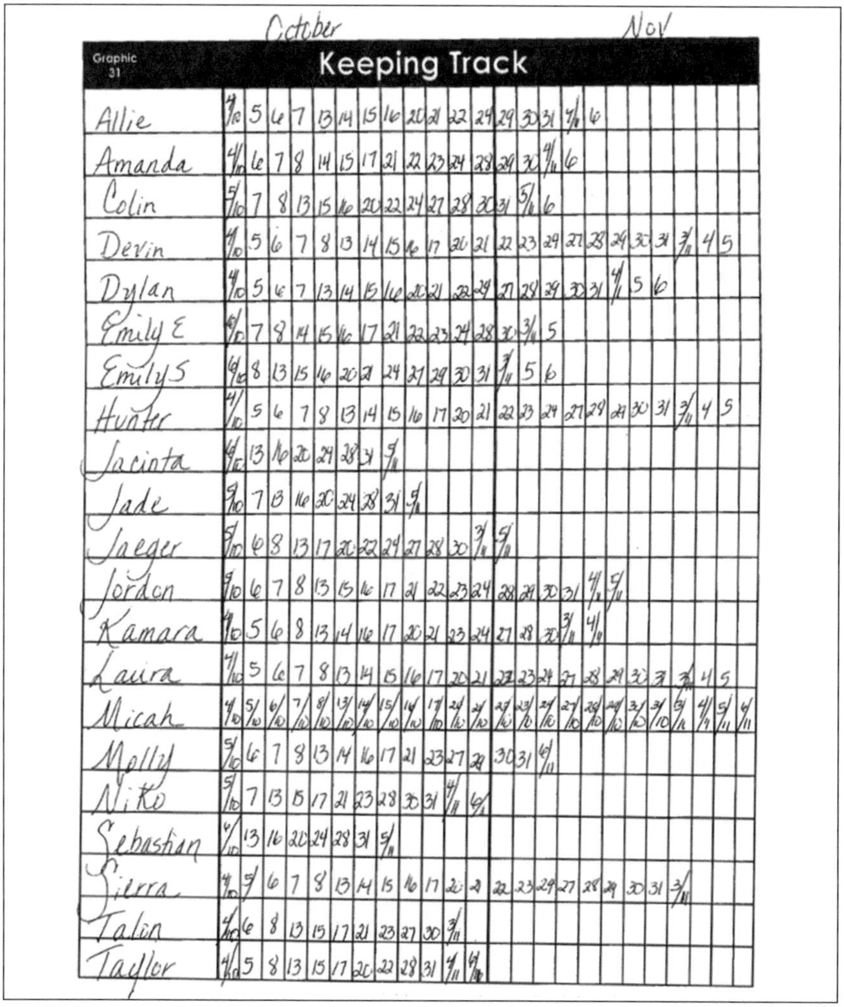

lots of boxes next to each child's name. They use the boxes to write the date they met with the child in either a small-group or individual session. We love using this checksheet, because a quick glance tells us which students we need to meet in a small group and/or conference.

Systems for Sharing Our Notes

One of the biggest challenges we are facing with formative assessment is finding time to communicate about our struggling readers. To comply with the regulations of Response to Intervention (RTI), we are providing additional tiers of targeted instruction for our struggling readers. At times, three or four different teachers may be providing services to one student. Research indicates the need for "relentless consistency" around core goals and practices (Fullan 2011) for our students. Recently we have been noticing a pattern when we analyze ongoing, formative notes with our intervention teams: some students have as many as twelve different learning goals across four teachers and may be trying to learn as many as three different cueing systems to decode unfamiliar words. We need to bring more cohesion to the instructional goals and strategies for these students so that they can experience the gradual release of responsibility. If their goals are changing with each tier of instruction, they never get a chance for extended modeling, scaffolding, and practice.

It is ideal if all the teachers providing instruction for a struggling reader can share the notes they are taking on these common goals. We are trying to find some ways to do just that.

Recording Data from Student Work

Notebook Entries and Reflections

We analyze student notebook entries to gather information on how students are applying the strategies we are teaching. In grades two through five we often use reading notebooks to have students set goals, reflect on their goals, document their thinking, and write in response to their reading. We use these notebooks during our whole-class, small-group, and individual lessons to assess what students have learned and what they need to learn next. Aimee Buckner in *Notebook Connections* (2009) shares how she uses notebooks as a tool to assess for teaching in the now. "When I assess children in my classroom, it's based on their performance over a period of time. I use a preponderance of evidence to determine their progress. This information, which is gathered on an ongoing basis, guides my teaching in the now. It shows me where kids are at present, where they were a few days or weeks ago, and what I need to do next to push them forward" (114). Using notebook entries and reflections as a tool to understand where students are in the process of learning helps us plan instruction to meet their needs and talk with them about the work they are doing to meet their goals. We record our observations in students' individual conferring notes or in our small-group notes.

Figure 5.8 shows an entry from Kelly's reading notebook. Kelly is recording possible themes as she reads each chapter, and recording the evidence from the book to support each one. Her work demonstrates her understanding of possible themes, and she is ready to learn how to connect them to determine the book's major theme or the author's message.

Figure 5.8
Kelly's Notebook
Entry

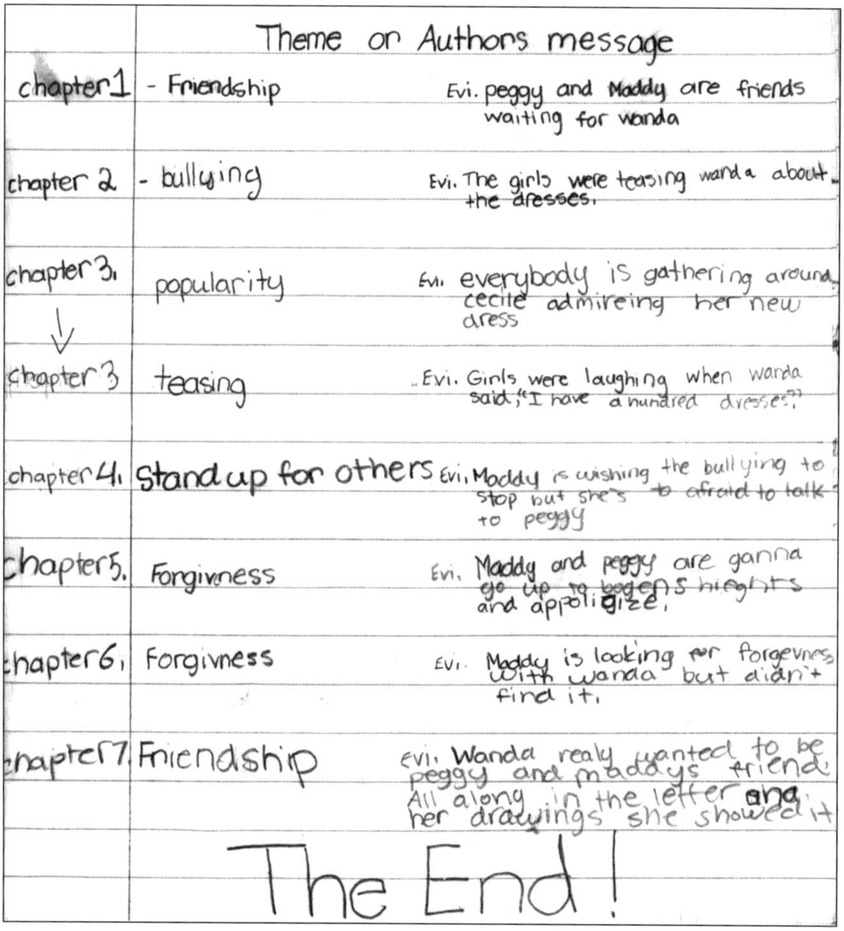

Here are our conferring notes after looking over Kelly's reading notebook.

Student Name: Kelly		
Goals: • Inferring the Theme		
Date/Title	**Observation and Instruction Notes**	**Instructional Goals: Next Steps to Meet Goals**
April 21 *Hundred Dresses* Notes on Theme	• She wrote possible themes for each chapter. • Does she know how to connect possible themes to determine the major themes of a text?	• Determine the major themes of the text by connecting the possible themes.

Book Logs

We found that we used to have to remind students constantly to record their reading on their logs. These conversations pushed us to think about the purpose of the book log and why we use logs in our daily lives. Students need to understand why they are logging their reading and how it is going to help them as readers. If they do not understand the purpose of the log, they may view it as laborious or a waste of their time. To use the log effectively, we need to adjust it to meet the reader's needs and goals. Once we make this shift, we find students are not only recording, but also setting goals based on the data collected in their logs. When we look at logs with students, we can track their progress in reading, set goals, and celebrate their successes. Sometimes we photocopy sections of a book log and add it to a student's conferring folder or just add the essential data we need from the log to our conferring notes.

Open/Constructed Response

Many state tests include a text passage to which the student is asked to write an open or constructed response. There are clear expectations and rubrics for these responses. When we work with students as they learn how to write this type of response, we often begin with a diagnostic assessment. We use student-constructed responses as diagnostic data to plan initial lessons and then continue to analyze writing samples to plan future lessons. We document what we notice about the students' responses in our conferring and small-group notes.

Voices from the Classroom

Gretchen Assesses in the Moment

Gretchen opens the whole-class lesson by saying, "Readers, we have been studying informational text and learning about how this genre is structured. Please turn and talk to your partner about what you are noticing about the features of this genre and how these features help you understand the text."

Gretchen listens to the partnerships and jots on the Messy Sheet what she hears the students discussing. She notes that students can name the text features and accurately identify them in the text, but cannot articulate how they help them understand what they are reading. She also makes a note to remind herself to follow up on these concepts during small-group and whole-group lessons.

During a small-group lesson, Gretchen models how she uses the headings to help her quickly determine where she can find the information she is looking for. She asks the students to explain how they would use the headings to find information about a topic they were researching. Again, she jots down notes on her small-group form to document what students say and understand about using text features. She notices once again that students can identify the features but are unclear about how to use them strategically. This confirms her hunch from the whole-class lesson.

During a conference with Brian, Gretchen asks what he is working on as a reader. Brian begins to show his research notes to her. She notices that he is copying random sentences from the text that are not connected to his research topic. Gretchen probes by asking, "Show me how you used the text features to take notes on your research topic." She then listens to Brian and documents in her conferring notes what he understands, what he is confused about, and what she is leaving him to work on as a reader. Brian is still confused about the features and is not accurately identifying those he has learned. What does Brian know about features? Is he using headings at all? Gretchen notes that she needs to continue to instruct Brian in how the genre of informational text is structured and how to use its features to find information.

Gretchen's focused questions and prompts during the whole-class, small-group, and individual lessons helps her identify important information about what to teach next to help her students continue to progress toward knowing how to use text structures and determining importance to understand text. ◄

Using Displays to Highlight Patterns in Our Summative, Diagnostic, and Formative Data

In Chapter 4 we discuss how we use displays to help us organize our data on our class or on a particular student when we have several sources to analyze and interpret. This process is done at different times and for different purposes. When we want to reflect on what a student or class has learned from a phase of instruction, we look at the data we have available and create a display to help us see what they have learned. This highlights summative patterns and typically happens at the end of an instructional phase. This same display is often then used diagnostically to highlight what readers need to learn. This type of analysis is done outside the process of teaching. We usually do this analysis during a data meeting or a planning meeting. This is when we gather all our data and take the time to puzzle through it and plan for our next instructional phase.

We also use displays formatively in the process of teaching to organize the observational notes and student work we are collecting every day in our classrooms. We want to use our notes and student work to make timely adjustments to our teaching, but those notes can pile up. Taking the time to go through all our notes and work samples on a nightly or weekly basis can be too time consuming. We would rather go for a run, garden, or do almost anything than spend our evenings looking through a huge stack of classroom notes.

We use the Messy Sheet "on the go" to help us display the patterns we notice in our observations and student work. As we see a new learning need emerge, we not only record it in our conferring and small-group notes but also write the corresponding concept or strategy in one of the circles on the Messy Sheet. We then list the names of the students who need instruction on that strategy under the circles. This allows us to see the needs of the students in our classroom on one sheet of paper. We do not need to flip through each section of our

Figure 5.9a
Messy Sheet at the End of an Instructional Period—Summative

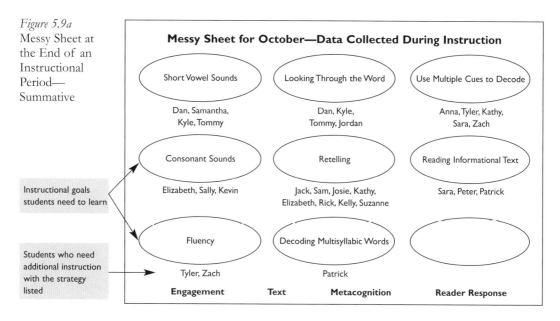

notebook and reread our conferring notes to plan our lessons. We have everything we need to inform our instruction on the Messy Sheet. If we need more specific data on a student or group of students, we refer to our conferring and small-group notes.

At the end of an instructional phase, we gather all the completed Messy Sheets and bring them to our data or planning meeting. We use them to reflect on the summative and diagnostic data they provide. These displays capture all the informal data for our class on one sheet so we can easily triangulate it with any formal, quantitative data we may have on our students as we plan for upcoming instruction.

For example, as we are teaching during the month of October we fill out the messy sheet in Figure 5.9a on the go. Each time we notice what a student needs to learn, we jot the concept in one of the circles and the student's name below the circle. This one sheet is a summary of our observations over the course of the month. At the end of October we look at these data with a summative perspective and we ask:

- What strategies did our students learn in October?
- What strategies do we need to teach in November?

As we look over this messy sheet, here are some of our observations:

- Since many students need to learn how to retell, we will teach this during whole-group and small-group lessons in November.

- We did not get to teach any fluency strategies in October, so we will teach a small group on fluency in November for the students who need those strategies.
- We notice that Patrick, Sara, and Peter need instruction on how to read informational text. We did not get to that in October. We have planned a nonfiction unit of study for December and will address those strategies then.
- Elizabeth, Sally, and Kevin now know more consonant sounds but still need reteaching of *Y, W, G, J.*
- Dan, Samatha, Kyle, and Tommy did learn their short vowel sounds this month.
- According to my conference notes, Dan and Kyle are looking through the word when figuring out an unfamiliar word, but Tommy and Jordan still need more practice.

Figure 5.9b is the messy sheet we created for the month of November. This messy sheet now gives us a diagnostic perspective because we used the data we gathered during the month of October and the curriculum to plan out our whole-class, small-group, and individual conferences for November.

Now that we have a plan for November, we create a messy sheet for collecting and recording data while we are teaching in November (Figure 5.9c). On this sheet we record some of the strategies we will be teaching so that we can add students' names as we observe them during the

Figure 5.9b
Messy Sheet at the Beginning of an Instructional Period—Diagnostic

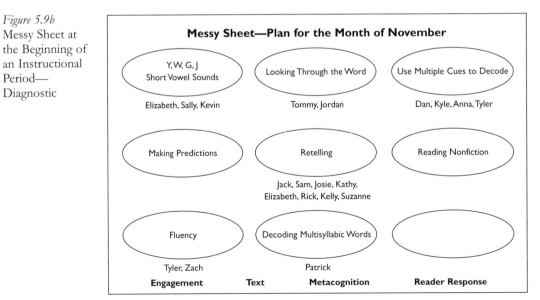

Figure 5.9c
Messy Sheet at the Beginning of an Instructional Period—Formative

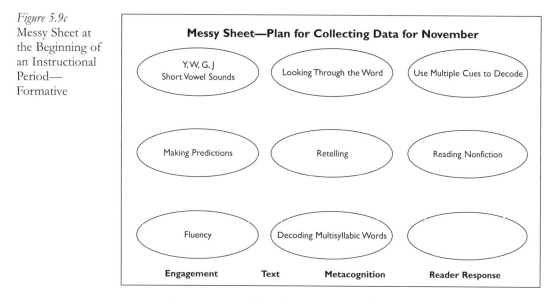

course of the month. We will collect these data as we teach, which makes this messy sheet a formative assessment tool. We will use the information we collect during November to plan instruction for December. We continue this process each month so we can use our formative data to choose instructional goals. If we have formal data during any month, we triangulate these formative data with that formal data.

***

Classroom assessments are powerful in terms of understanding our students in the context of learning. We have made a commitment to bringing the process of triangulating into our instruction—authentically, every day. It is just what we do when we teach. This assessment stance in our teaching not only gives us the essential information we need in the moment but also engages our students in the process of learning. Daniel Pink's research demonstrates that "the secret to high performance and satisfaction—at work, at school, and at home—is the deeply human need to direct our own lives, to learn and create new things, and to do better by ourselves and our world" (2011, 3). When we include instruction in our assessment process, students begin to have a role in assessment. Teaching is dynamic, and teachable moments are not something we can plan for. They are fleeting opportunities that must be sensed and seized by the teacher. When our students know we are listening, they begin engaging, and this creates a learning environment that provides opportunities to listen, reflect, and learn. When this happens, it is truly magical.

THE STORIES WE CARRY

Using Assessment to Adjust Our Teaching to the Student's Needs

Ana was a first grader. She began the year on benchmark on two different assessments—the DRA and the DIBELS Nonsense Word Fluency. In November she began intervention because of her lack of progress. In January she continued to meet or exceed benchmark on the DIBELS Nonsense Word Fluency, but showed no progress on the DRA (still an instructional Level 3). In March, she still did not demonstrate any progress on the DRA, despite having received extensive intervention over five months. Ana continued to receive the same intervention method several times a week across two tiers of instruction, but no changes were made to the instructional methodology even though she was not responding to the research-based intervention. By May of first grade Ana was still an instructional level 3 based on the DRA. While the team struggled and debated over Ana's diagnosis and how to "label" her difficulties with reading, one teacher, Deb, decided to look beyond the numbers and ask, "Why is Ana performing differently on different assessments?" and "What would happen if we instructed Ana differently?"

Deb triangulated Ana's reading data with her formal evaluation (Figure S5.1). Ana demonstrated strengths in listening comprehension and oral language. She also demonstrated above-average strengths in decoding nonsense words and words in isolation. "Why can she decode in isolation but not in context?" Deb wondered. All of Ana's

Figure S5.1
Using a
Display to
Triangulate
Ana's Formal
Reading Data

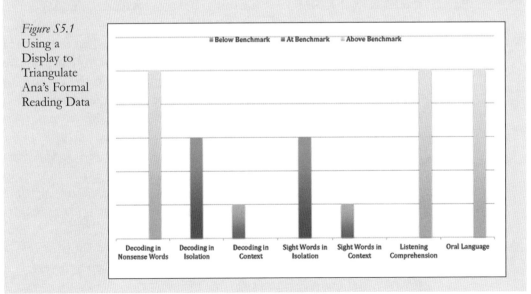

instruction up to this point had been on isolated skills and with controlled texts that did not reflect natural language patterns or an authentic narrative structure. Deb asked, "What if we used authentic text with Ana? What if we focused on some meaning strategies with her? What if our instruction focused on teaching her to use her strengths as well as develop her weaknesses?"

After two weeks of a different instructional approach, Ana began to demonstrate progress (Figure S5.2). After three weeks of instruction she was assessed using a running

Figure S5.2 Ana's Conferring Notes, Week 1

CONFERRING NOTES

Student Name: Ana

Goals:
- Preview the book—what is this book about?
- Read the picture—what words might I find?

Date/Title	Observation and Instruction Notes	Instructional Goals: Next Steps to Meet Goals
4/29 Level B *At the Park*	• never looks at the picture • stops at difficulty and looks at me • shrugs • waits me out	• teach strategy step by step • preview • look at picture • focus on why readers do this
4/30 Level C *I Play Soccer*	• looked at strategy card but did not use it • read the picture when prompted • previewed text after I modeled with yesterday's book	• see if she previews the text without prompting next session
5/4 Level C *Cold*	• previewed the text on her own • used strategy card on her own • nice job reading the pictures— taking time to look, think, and even "talk" through the pictures	• model asking "Does that make sense?" • cross-check with the picture
5/6 Level D RR *A Special Day* 100% accuracy	• only using first letter as cue • really using the strategy card well • prompts herself • not looking at me	• try transferring her "tap it out" skill strategically to text • add to strategy card • teach "skip it"

Engagement   Text   Metacognition   Reader Response

record. Ana scored 95 percent accuracy with excellent comprehension at a Level E. When Deb analyzed the running record, she noted that when faced with a problem, Ana still resorted to visual strategies (Figure S5.3), but the decoding in authentic text did not match her scores in decoding nonsense words and words in isolation. Why would that be?

Figure S5.3 Ana's Fountas and Pinnell Benchmark Assessment System Results

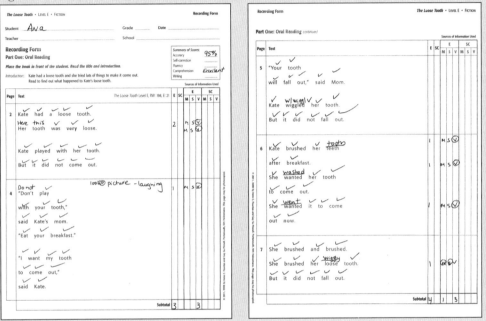

Deb continued having Ana focus on meaning strategies for her first attempt, but then also chose a goal that had her using her decoding skills strategically in authentic texts. She focused on modeling how a reader uses those skills in the moment when reading. After a week of this instruction, this is what her reading looked like (see Figure S5.4). Ana had progressed four levels in five weeks.

After being stalled at the same level for almost a year, Ana had developed some ineffective strategies. When facing an unknown word, her first strategy was to look at the adult, then shrug, then rub her eyes, and then put her head down. Deb talked to Ana about what she was noticing about her behaviors when she faced a problem. She made a strategy bookmark for Ana so that she could cue herself what to do when she came to an unknown word. Deb used a strategy inventory to assess Ana's use of strategies unprompted and used it to focus her instruction (see Figure S5.5).

Figure S5.4 Ana's Conferring Notes, Weeks 2–3

CONFERRING NOTES

Student Name: Ana

Goals:
- Skip it and see what makes sense.
- Tap it out—flip the vowel.
- Chunk it.

Date/Title	Observation and Instruction Notes	Instructional Goals: Next Steps to Meet Goals
5/7 Level E (RR) *Sister, Sister* 97% Accuracy	• excellent comprehension • laughing • talking to the book	• confusion around what a vowel is • teach vowel names and sounds
5/11 Level E	• vowels—what are they? • skip it—modeled and tried together • using meaning well	• vowels • skip it
5/12 Level E	• vowels • Skip it—she cross-checks much better when she skips it, but always needs to be prompted to do that.	• skip it • vowels • tap it out on cross-check
5/14 Level E	• tapping it out nicely with nonverbal signal—not from strategy list • short vowels getting better • using skip it when prompted	• cross-check—skip/tap
5/19 Level E	• tapping it out nicely with nonverbal signal—not from strategy list • short vowels getting better • using skip it when prompted	• cross-check—skip/tap • long vowels
5/22 Level F (RR) *Car Wash* 94% Accuracy Excellent Comprehension		

Engagement   Text   Metacognition   Reader Response

Figure S5.5 Ana's Strategy Inventory

Name: Ana
Date: 5/25
Book: *Buzz Said the Bee*
Level: F

Strategy Inventory

Read the picture	+++++++++++++++++++++++++++
Chunk it	
Tap it out	++++++++++++++
Skip it—What makes sense?	++
Flip the vowel	
Self-correct	+++++++++++
Monitor—comments/flipping/laughing	+++++
Other	

Ana's lack of progression over the year also affected her disposition as a reader. She did not view herself as a reader and could not name any books she liked. Deb decided to use these data to plan instruction to help Ana develop her identity as a reader. They explored different types of texts, set reading goals at home, discussed readers' habits, and added a reader response goal to her school goals.

After three months, Ana had progressed to instructional Level G and could name many books and series that she loved! She was still working on building a reading habit at home and viewing herself as "smart" and a "reader." Formal assessments continued to document that Ana had difficulty processing, retrieving information with automaticity, and sequencing sounds to decode in context. She continued to need and received intervention in these areas of weakness, but now she was doing that in a text level within the range of her grade level. Deb used assessment data to ask questions and dig deeper. She adjusted her instruction and watched how Ana responded, and then adjusted her instruction again. Assessment and instruction were happening simultaneously. Assessment was the tool that helped Deb design instruction to meet Ana's needs as a reader.

CHAPTER 6

The Student's Role in Assessment

99

The heart of formative assessment is finding the edge of students' learning and helping them to take up possibilities of growth. Assessment isn't formative if it doesn't influence learning in a positive way. Formative assessment isn't only the teacher's responsibility. However, it is the teacher's responsibility to ensure that students know how and are disposed to take up their responsibility for formative assessment.

—Peter Johnston, *Opening Minds* (2012)

▶ Tammy arrives for her session with a small group of struggling readers. Ben comes in, drops his things on the table, slumps into the chair, and sighs with frustration. Tammy asks, "What's wrong?"

He replies, "I hate coming here. Why do I have to come to this group? I don't know why I have to come here."

Tammy listens and then asks, "Do you want to know why?" He sits up a bit straighter and nods his head. Tammy then shares his assessment data with him and explains what she is noticing about him as a reader. This student has no idea he is reading two grade levels below benchmark. Tammy wonders to herself, *How can someone get better at something if he doesn't know how he is doing?*

Ben asks, "What does this chart mean?" Tammy explains that the chart illustrates that he is having difficulty decoding multisyllabic words and inferring the meaning of texts.

"How can I get better at that?" he asks. "What do I need to do?" Tammy explains the focus of the small group and how it will help him. She also explains the weekly assessment she is using and the notebook assignment he is doing, and how both of those will help them monitor his progress toward his goal.

"So this will help me read better?" Ben asks.

"It should, but you need to let me know what is helpful and what is challenging. When you tell me how it is going for you, it helps me change the way I am teaching to help you more. That is why I am asking you to keep track of your strategies in your notebook."

"That makes sense. I thought you just wanted to keep me busy during reading so I would not talk to my friends so much."

Tammy laughs and says, "Well, talking to your friends will not help you meet your goal, but I should have explained the assignment better. Let's get started." ◀

Researchers Robert Marzano and Mark Haystead in *Making Standards Useful in the Classroom* (2008) concluded that if teachers explicitly shared in each lesson what students were going to learn, why they were going to learn it, and how it would help them as learners, student understanding would increase by 80 percent. This is powerful research that can be applied to any curriculum, program, or set of standards. We find that when we explain the purpose of a lesson to our students and tell them how it will help them as readers, they have a better understanding of how to use the strategies being taught when they are reading independently. When we are explicit with our students about the purpose behind our teaching and give them a window into our thinking about how it will support their reading development, it helps set them up for learning. Susan M. Brookhart, author of *How to Give Effective Feedback to Your Students* (2008), says, "Once they feel they understand what to do and why, most students develop a feeling that they have control over their own learning" (2).

We believe it is our job to let students in on our beliefs about teaching and learning. They should know that we believe all students can achieve high expectations and that we will set and monitor goals toward those expectations. They should understand that we believe assessment is more than a number and that we will be observing the progress and the challenges of their work through their notes, their journal responses, and the feedback they give us about how their learning is going for them. They need to know that we believe that assessment is inseparable from instruction. Instructional time is not a time for them to simply listen to us talk or read aloud but to actively engage, reflect, and share in the process of learning. Students can do that only if they are clearly aware of our instructional goals, their instructional goals, and the steps they need to take to progress toward them. We share our plan of instruction with them and talk with them about how we are using what they are telling us about their learning as assessment to move them toward the next step of understanding.

Peter Johnston's work around the importance of words in the classroom pushed our thinking about how to use language to truly engage our students in this process of instruction and assessment. His dynamic-learning framework (Figure 6.1), influenced by Dweck's (2006) growth mind-set theory, asserts that ability or intelligence is something that grows with learning and reflects the social-constructive theory of dialogic teaching. In these theories or frameworks, it is the process of learning—how readers do something—that is most

Figure 6.1
Dynamic-
Learning Beliefs
and Fixed-
Performance
Beliefs

Dynamic-Learning Beliefs and Fixed-Performance Beliefs	
Belief System Frames	
Dynamic-Learning Frame	**Fixed-Performance Frame**
The more you learn, the smarter you get. You can change your mind, your smartness, and who you become.	People have fixed traits, such as smartness, intelligence, and personality, that they cannot change.
Learning takes time and effort, so trying hard is valued.	Learning happens quickly for smart people, so trying hard is not valued; if you have to try hard, you probably aren't smart.
The most important information is *how* someone did (or could do) something, because that's what we can learn from.	The most important information is whether one is successful. It shows who is smart and more valuable. *How* one succeeds is irrelevant. (Cheating and lying can be justifiable routes to success.)
The goal is to learn as much as you can.	The goal is to look as smart as you can.
Frequent success without trying hard indicates choosing activities that are too easy to learn from.	Frequent success without trying is an indicator of one's (fixed) ability and value.
Problems/challenges/errors are to be expected if a person is taking on challenge—which is valued (even experts/authors make mistakes).	Problems/challenges/errors are indicators of one's intellectual ability.
Challenging and novel activities are engaging.	Challenging and novel activities are risky/stressful.
Collaboration is important and success requires it, along with interest and efforts to comprehend. Seeking help is sensible after exhausting one's own resources.	Competition is important and success requires ability and a competitive focus. Seeking help is evidence of one's intellectual inadequacy.
Greater competence means being able to take on new challenges and greater opportunity to help others.	Greater competence means being smarter and therefore better (and more valuable) than others, and potentially having power over others.

important to us as teachers. Vygotsky watched what students did when they were faced with problems. Getting an idea about how students get started, how they use the strategies they have been taught, and what they do when the going gets tough gives an important perspective on what they can apply on their own as they are learning. We want our students to talk with us and share the challenges, confusions, and problems they encounter as they are learning. When they share this information, they help us customize our instruction to meet their needs.

Feedback, especially specific and immediate feedback, is essential to these frameworks. In this view of achievement, assessment is essential to learning and students need to be aware of how our feedback affects their process of learning or "how learning is going." "Effective feedback requires that a person has a goal, takes action to achieve the goal, and receives goal-related information about his or her actions. Learners are often unclear about the specific goal of the task or lesson, so it is crucial to remind them about the goal" (Wiggins 2012, 2). We have been thinking a lot about the role of the student in assessment. How are we sharing data with our students? Are we creating a culture that supports the use of data in a dynamic-learning framework? Do our students talk about their strategic processes and provide us feedback about how learning is going for them? Have we shared with our students that we view their feedback as formative assessment that influences our instruction?

Black and William (1998) studied the effect of formative assessment, from both teacher and student, on achievement and found that it is an essential component of effective teaching. Their research concluded that in order to see this positive effect, our profession needs to improve the quality of the feedback we give our students and the feedback our students give us and themselves. "When anyone is trying to learn, feedback about the effort has three elements: recognition of the desired goal, evidence about present position, and some understanding of a way to close the gap between the two. All three must be understood to some degree by anyone before he or she can take action to improve understanding" (Black and William 1998, 6). This research supports our beliefs that students need to be aware of their goals and their role in providing us with feedback about how the process of learning is going for them. Our readers need to know that we are listening, watching, and expecting them to grow, learn, make errors, set goals, and reflect on the entire process. They need to know that we view learning in a dynamic framework.

We share this dynamic-learning framework with our students so they are aware that learning takes time and that when true learning is happening, challenges, confusion, and mistakes are inevitable. We document all students' goals with them on their conferring notes and help them make a plan for their learning. We talk to our students about how they will work on these goals for several weeks and tell them we need their feedback on which aspects of the strategies we are teaching are working well and which are causing confusion for them. We want them to understand the role of formative assessment in their learning process. Our students need to understand that assessment for learning is not evaluative but a critical component of the process of learning.

Voices from the Classroom

Discussing Goals with Readers

Before Karen begins conferring with Sophia, one of her fourth graders, she looks at her conferring notes to remember Sophia's instructional goal. Her notes show that Sophia was learning how to record her thinking about the main character. This information gives Karen a starting point for the conference. She begins the conference by asking Sophia to show her and explain how she has been taking notes to help her understand the main character. "Sophia, you have been working on taking notes about the main character in a way that will help you understand, talk about, and write about your character. How has that been going for you?"

"I've been writing a lot of things down, but I'm not sure if I'm writing the right things, and I don't know where to put everything. Once I have an idea about my character, I don't know where to put it."

"Okay, so it sounds like you're noticing things about your character, but you're not sure which things are important and you would like to work on finding a way to organize your notes. Those are two ideas, both really important, to help you meet your goal. Which idea do you think would be most helpful for us to work on today?"

"Maybe organizing my notes would be the first thing. Right now everything is such a mess, I can't even begin to think about what information is important."

"That sounds like a plan." ◄

If we want our students to value our feedback and view it as constructive rather than evaluative, then it must be tied clearly to their stated learning goals. Katie Rapp describes feedback as part of an assessment system that is completely open, with no surprises.

> Teachers should present students with a list of achievement standards that they must master to be successful in the course of study. And students should understand that, at some point, they will be held accountable through a rigorous assessment, which will allow them to demonstrate their mastery of these standards. This summative assessment, which might culminate in test scores and grades, is completely separate from the formative process, which is assessment for learning. Assessment for learning includes feedback for learning, and feedback should focus on a learning target. Feedback tells students where they are on the continuum. They understand how they are progressing toward the goal and where they need to improve so that they can continue to progress. In this way, students generate their own feedback and become partners with teachers in setting goals for what comes next in their own learning. This kind of high-quality, descriptive feedback turns the 'keys to the kingdom' over to students and shows them that they are in control of their learning. (2012, 2)

In order for this to all come together, we need to give our students some background on assessment, how we use it to help them grow, and the importance of their role in this process.

Assessment Literacy

If students understand the how and why behind assessments, they can approach them with a sense of purpose, inquiry, and understanding. If Zachary had assessment literacy and understood why he was being asked to draw his self-portrait again and how his teacher planned to use this information, he may have been more engaged in the process and put forth more effort. We are not suggesting that we teach our elementary readers complex assessment-related knowledge, but we do think it is essential for students to understand our purpose in assessing them and to share the results of the assessments in a manner that helps them set goals and grow as readers.

When we are meeting with our students in conferences or small groups, we share assessment data with them and talk with them about what we notice and what questions come to mind when we look at their data. We focus on the same questions with our students that we use when we are building our own assessment literacy:

- What is the purpose?
- What method did we use?
- What type of data do we have?

Purpose

Our readers need to know why we are assessing them and how we plan to use the information. For example, we might say the following:

> *"So, readers, today I am going to begin assessing during our workshop time. During this assessment, I am going to ask you to read a text and then talk with me about this text. It will be like a conference but a little bit longer. This will help me find you books that you will love and that will help me teach you the strategies you need to grow as a reader. These assessments help me get to know you as a reader. As I get to know you better, I will be able to teach you better. After the assessment, we will pick some new books together and choose some goals to work on over the next few weeks. Does anyone have any questions?"*

When we share data from an assessment with our readers, we want them to know if we are measuring what they have learned, what they knew before instruction, or how they have responded to the instruction we are currently providing. This information will explain why students are learning specific strategies. Readers especially need to understand how we are using formative assessments authentically every day and their role in providing these essential data to us. We want our students to understand that their responses, behaviors, and work are a type of assessment data. They need to be aware of the importance of these data to the timely adjustments we make to our instruction. When students realize that we analyze and use this information continually, they begin to engage more in the work they are doing and reflect more on the process of their learning.

Method

We find that our students are very aware of the formal assessments we are administering. Students know when "the test" is approaching or when it is a formal assessment window for their grade level. Some educators really worry about the stress these assessments place on children and worry that they will become anxious about testing. Others take the view that formal assessments are just a normal aspect of school. Which message do we send when we hang "Quiet: Testing in Progress" signs around the school, ask students to get extra sleep for the test, or cancel homework the week of these tests? Are we giving more value to formal assessments? If we value informal assessments equally, shouldn't students come to school prepared to do their best learning every day, not just on the days of "the test"?

We talk with our students about both methods and why we use them. We try not to place more value on one or the other. We want them to understand why formal assessments are administered differently from informal assessments and why we use informal assessments more often. We share data from both types with our students and discuss how we use it to help us plan instructional goals for them.

Type of Data

Although we never want to define a reader by a number, we do often have data in the form of numbers on our students. When we share quantitative assessment data with them, we always ask them to provide qualitative data by reflecting on what they think about that number. Their reflection gives us information critical to understanding why they may have performed a particular way on a quantitative assessment. Their behaviors and reflections on the process of learning provide us the in-depth description we need to teach them effectively. How we ask these questions and the language we use to discuss the process of learning is critical to the quality and quantity of qualitative data we gather in our classrooms. This is where the growth mind-set or the dynamic framework of learning is essential. We want our readers to know we are not solely looking at performance when we analyze assessments. It is the process they describe that is the most valuable data for our instructional decisions. Following is an example of gathering qualitative data.

"So, Michael, I want to talk with you about the assessment we did yesterday. Remember when I had you read those words yesterday? What did you notice about doing that?"

"I didn't do well on that, did I?"

"Why do you ask?"

"Well, I couldn't read them. I didn't know the words, and there was nothing to help me."

"What would have been helpful to you if you did not know the words?"

"If you could put those words in a sentence, then I could read them. That really helps me. When the words are by themselves, I don't know how to read them."

"That is really important information you are sharing with me. It really helps me know how to help you. This assessment shows us whether you have strategies to decode long words that are unfamiliar to you. It sounds like you typically use the story or the sentence to figure out those words. I can teach you some strategies so you can figure out the word more quickly without the sentence. Do you think that would be helpful?"

"Yes. It takes me a really long time to reread all the sentences every time I don't know a word."

"Should we make that a goal for the next few weeks?"

"Yes. I'll add it to my goal form."

We think students need an opportunity to look at their assessments and think about what they notice and what questions they have. Susan M. Brookhart, in *Advancing Formative Assessment in Every Classroom: A Guide for Instructional Leaders* (2009), suggests that teachers provide opportunities for students to participate in generating feedback rather than acting as passive receivers. For example, she says, "Rather than telling the student all the things you notice about his or her work, start by asking, 'What are you noticing about this?' or 'Why did you decide to do it this way?'" (15). Following are some of the assessments we share with our students to build their assessment literacy.

Running Records

Before we begin administering a running record, we explain to our students what type of assessment it is, why we are using it, and how we use the information in the classroom. We tell them that as we listen to them read, we are going to take notes that show which strategies they have learned to apply independently and which ones they are ready to learn next. Once the assessment is finished, we explain what we notice to the students. We begin by celebrating their strengths and showing them where in the running record we noticed them using the strategies they have been learning. Then we tell them the strategies they are ready to learn next and show them how we know that based on the running record. We then set and document goals with the students.

Retelling

We use some assessments, like the DRA2, that require a formal retelling. The first time we use this assessment with a student, we use it diagnostically. Once we have administered the assessment, we explain to the student the assessment's expectation for a complete retelling. We then show the student how he or she retold the story and how he or she scored. Students typically become very interested and want us to know they could have told us more, used proper names, and retold in sequence if they had known that that was what we wanted them to do. They often ask us if they can try it again. We think this example is important because our students need to understand the expectations in order to do well on an assessment. Many students are confused by retellings. In most of life's contexts, including a classroom, we assume shared understanding, but with a retelling, the student has to assume the teacher has never heard the story even though he or she was sitting there when the student read it to him or her. Once students know what is expected of them, they are more engaged in subsequent instruction that focuses on strategies to remember and retell.

Book Logs

In Chapter 5, we discuss the importance of students understanding why they are logging their reading and how it is going to help them as readers. When talking to students about book logs, we share our own logs and some samples that students have used in the past. We show them how to make personal book logs in their reading notebooks to help them track their progress in reading, set goals, and celebrate their successes. We find that when students either select their own book logs or actually create them, they have more ownership over the process and use the data to reflect on their growth. Figure 6.2 shows Andrew's independent reading log.

Unit of Study: Launching Independent Reading

Anchor Lesson: 11. Keeping a log of titles and genres

Independent Reading Log   Name: Andrew

Date	Title	Pages Read
6/10/08	The Kinapped King	21
6/12/08	Hank Zipper #11	13
6/11/08	"	8
6/13/08	"	12
6/14/08	"	
6/15/08	Once Upon a Time in Japan	13
6/16/08	Hank Zipper	14
6/17/08	Once upon a time in Japan	10
6/20/08	Hank Zipper	10
6/21/08	"	13
6/22/08	"	14

Unit of Study: Launching Independent Reading

Anchor Lesson: 11. Keeping a log of titles and genres

Independent Reading Log   Name: Andrew

Date	Title	Pages Read
6/24/08	Hank Zipper #12	24
6/25/08	"	16
6/26/08	"	20
6/27/08	"	38
6/28/08	"	88
6/29/08	Who was Anne F (Anne Frank)	34
6/30/08	"	25
7/1/08	"	42
7/2/08	Hank Zipper	20
7/3/08	"	20
7/4/08	"	25

Figure 6.2
Andrew's
Reading Log

Following is a conversation we might have with Andrew about his book log:

"So, Andrew, let's take a look at your books logs. On June 12 we met and talked about your reading. You reflected that you weren't really reading a lot at home, and with summer approaching, you thought that would be a good goal for you—to read more at home. So let's take a look at your log from home. What do you notice?"

"I notice that at first I didn't read more pages, but I did read more often. I started reading almost every day. Once I got in the habit, I set a new goal to read more pages each day. I set that goal on June 24."

"How did that work out for you?"

"Good. I started reading for longer amounts of time, and I more than doubled the number of pages on some days."

"What do you think is your next step as a reader? How do you feel about the work you have been doing?"

"I think I met my goal, and reading at home is becoming more of a habit. I am getting tired of the series I'm in. I think my next goal is to try a new series, or author, or genre."

"Do you think you will use this log or make a new one to track that goal?"

"I don't know. How would I change it?"

"I could show you some samples. It might help for you to keep track of the genres or authors you are reading so you can see if you are trying new things. You could also have a column to reflect on whether you liked the new genre, author, or series."

"That's a cool idea. I'd like to see some samples."

Notebook Entries and Response

In Chapter 5, we share how we use reading notebooks with our students. We agree with Franki Sibberson and Karen Szymusiak:

> Although we do not give written tests or use end-of-chapter comprehension questions, we do want a place for our students to record and reflect on their growth as readers. These notebooks give us the information we need to plan whole-class lessons as well as small-group and individual instruction. We refer to them continuously to analyze and assess student needs. (2003, 36)

These notebooks are a place for our students to take notes, document evidence to support their ideas, grow their thinking, prepare for book clubs, log their reading, set goals, and follow through on assignments. We typically begin our small-group or individual lessons by asking students to open their notebooks to the section they have been using to document their thinking for the instructional goal we are about to address. This serves two purposes: (1) It provides wonderful assessment data about what the students have and have not done since our last session (we love the ones who cannot even find their notebooks in the black hole of their desks) and (2) it sends a message that we are holding students accountable for their part in learning by checking what they are doing in their notebooks.

Once we collect these formative data, we can begin to model for students how to lift the quality of what they are doing and model the strategy they working on as readers. We show students our observations about what they are doing and talk to them about what we think they are ready to learn next. This analysis gives them meaningful feedback and helps them set goals. Following is an example.

"Catharine, I had a chance to look at some of your responses in your notebook last night and the notes you have been taking as you are reading. You

have been working on collecting evidence as you read to support your thesis around theme and then trying to incorporate that evidence into your writing. What have you noticed about doing this?"

"Well, I think I've been doing a better job at keeping the notes."

"What do you mean by better—can you show in your notebook what has been working well for you?"

Catharine opens her notebook to a section of note taking. "Here, I organized my notes so that this section is just the thoughts I am having about the theme, this section has quotes to support my theme, and this section is my thoughts about the message in the book—you know, like what it pushes me to think about in my life."

"How has that been helping you?"

"Well, for one, when I go to write my response, I know right where my quotes are to support my thinking. It has helped me put that evidence into my writing."

"That's great. I noticed that in your writing as well. Right here, in your response, it was very clear how the evidence supported your thinking. Do you think this goal is one to keep working on, or is there something else you want to focus on?"

"I think I need to keep working on this goal. Right now I am very focused on doing it and I want to make it easier for myself so it doesn't take so much time or thought away from my reading."

"That is a really important thing to notice. We want this to help you think, not cause you to lose focus in your reading. Why don't you keep working on it and jot down how it's going? Let's meet in a day or two and discuss what you are noticing."

Open/Constructed Response

In Chapter 5 we explain how we often begin with a diagnostic assessment when we are teaching our students to write open or constructed responses. We give them a passage and question and have them write their response before we have provided instruction or shared the structure of this kind of test item. We do this so we can involve our students in the process of analysis and goal setting. After they have taken the assessment, we share the rubric and the exemplars with them. The first response is typically, "We could do that. We just didn't know that was what you wanted." Our students understand the purpose of this diagnostic assessment and help us construct a plan to improve their response to meet the rubric.

Voices from the Classroom

Building Assessment Literacy with Students

It was midyear and time for me to begin assessing my students. I needed to make a plan to get the assessments finished effectively and efficiently. "Which ones do I need to give?" I looked through my assessment binder and saw it was the DRA2 and the DIBELS Oral Reading Fluency. "I think it will be quickest if I just assess each student with both tools rather than all the students with one tool and then all the students with the other tool. That way I'll interrupt each student only once."

The next day I began assessing. "My plan is working like a charm!" I say to myself. I had assessed three students already. As I began assessing my next student, I noticed Harry, who sat near my assessment table, listening in. "I better do him soon so he'll stop being distracted and get back to work."

Harry sauntered over and took a seat. I was about to begin the first assessment with him. He stopped me and said, "Hold it. Is this the assessment when I have to read as fast as I can and *not* remember what I read or is this the assessment I have to read fast and remember?"

I stopped dead in my tracks. I had been giving these assessments for years and had never thought of them that way before.

"Why do you ask?"

"Well, I use different strategies depending on which one it is."

Wow, I thought. Do we want to send a message that sometimes readers don't think or remember? "Harry, you have asked a really good question. I am going to think about your question and talk to some other teachers about it. Then I will get back to you."

"Am I going to read now? I want to know which strategy to use."

"You know what? I think today I would rather hear how you use different strategies for each. If you help me understand that, then you will help me think about these assessments and how I can use them better in our classroom. Your feedback about these two assessments is really helpful, and I want to share it with the other teachers." ◄

Triangulating Data

Triangulating data is our best safeguard for preventing a fixed-performance framework (see Figure 6.1). When we triangulate our data, we are always looking at different types, sources, and intervals of data to support a dynamic-learning framework. We want our readers to know that we use data to uncover and understand, not to label and define. We also want our readers to know that they provide one of the best sources of data for triangulating. If "eighty percent of the time, a diagnosis can be made on history—the diagnosis is in the story," then we need to make sure we are talking to our readers about how they think learning is going for them. Their insights and thoughts on the process of learning often give us the information we need to illuminate, confirm, or dispute what we learned from an initial analysis of one piece of data. When they know this, they understand their role in assessment and in the process of learning. They come to expect us to ask questions, observe, and analyze their work. We also find that once our readers understand their role in triangulating data, they begin to engage in this process themselves. They begin to analyze, question, and assess their own learning.

Showing our students the displays we use to collect and analyze data is often helpful in getting them talking about their data. We like to begin by having them look at the display, share what they notice, and tell us what questions come to mind for them when they analyze the display. This allows them to be in control of the process and think about why the data are showing what they are showing. Our readers are often in the best position to explain the why behind the data, but first we have to engage them in the dialogue. Jane E. Pollock, author of *Feedback: The Hinge That Joins Teaching and Learning* (2012), highlights the importance of helping students self-regulate and recommends having them create goal-accounting templates so that they can track their daily effort toward meeting their goal and generate their own feedback. Displays are a great way to begin a conversation about how learning is going without putting students on the defensive. Following are some conversations with students and examples of displays that they create, analyze, and use to set and reflect on their reading goals.

***

"Adam, you set a goal last month to increase your reading rate. I took the timings you did and put them in a display (Figure 6.3). What do you notice?"

"Wow. My rate really did get better. My goal was 140, and I am pretty close. I bet if I stuck with this goal I could make it in the next few weeks."

"How do you think it is helping you as a reader?"

"Well, I think it is just keeping me focused. Sometimes I lose focus

Figure 6.3
Adam's Fluency
Graph

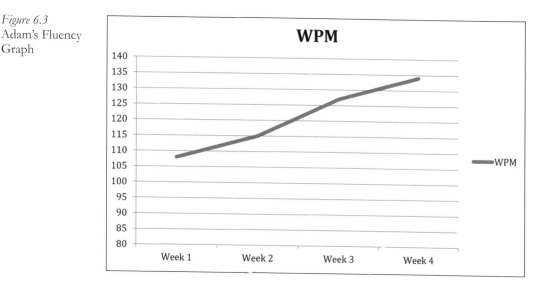

when I'm reading, and I think that slows me down. I didn't really try to read faster. I think I was just more focused when I was reading. Then the more I got into the story, the faster it went."

"Do you think you are understanding and thinking while you're reading? We read to think about the author's message, the characters, or a topic. I want to make sure you are still doing that work as a reader."

"I think that's also getting better. Maybe that can be my goal after I hit 140. Can I use this display to track the next few weeks?"

***

Figure 6.4
Data Wall

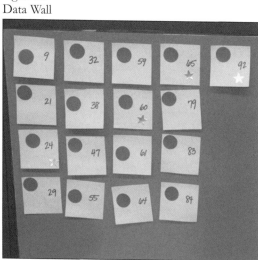

"So, Sarah, I wanted to show you something. This is a data wall (Figure 6.4). It helps me understand what each student needs as a reader. When I look at your data I have a lot of questions. I wanted to hear what you think about your data. Let me explain what the wall is showing. You are number 60. You are in the red section and have a red dot because on our classroom assessments and in the work you do during reading workshop you are having a difficult time. Would you agree?"

"Yes. Reading is really hard. I'm not good at it. I never have been a good reader. Why do I have a gold star on my number?"

"That's interesting. The gold star means

that you scored quite well on our state test. According to that test, you're quite a strong reader. What do you think about that? What questions does it make you ask?"

"I don't know. Maybe I'm not such a bad reader. Can I see that test?"

***

"Tyler, as I watched you read today I made a strategy inventory display (Figure 6.5). What do you notice?"

"I notice that I read the picture a lot and I skip it a lot."

"So what happens after you skip it?"

"I just skip it. I don't go back to figure it out."

"Is that working for you as a reader?"

"Not really. There are a lot of words I'm not reading."

"What is hard for you? What do you think would help?"

"Well, once I go back I'm not sure what to do. I still don't know it, so I just go on."

"Do you think some strategies to tap it out or chunk it might help?"

"That would be a good goal. I don't do that very much."

"Great. Let's put those as your goals and focus on them for the next few weeks. How will you remember your goals?"

Figure 6.5
Tyler's Strategy
Inventory

Name: Tyler
Date: 3/31
Book: *Teeny Tiny Woman*
Level: F

Strategy Inventory

Read the picture	+++++++++++++++++++++++++
Chunk it	+++++
Tap it out	+
Skip it—What makes sense?	+++++++++++++++++++++++
Flip the vowel	
Self-correct	
Monitor—comments/flipping/laughing	
Other	

***

"Liz, you have been using this display (Figure 6.6) to keep track of your goals. How is it working for you? What do you notice about yourself as a reader?"

"It has really helped me to write my goals down and reflect on them each week. Sometimes I forget my goal or just think I need to work on it for a day or two. This display helps me stay focused and do the work I need to do. It also helps me realize my next goal. Since I'm reflecting on my progress each week, it's easy to determine my next goals."

Figure 6.6
Liz's Reading
Goals

Week	Goal 1	Goal 2	Date I Met My Goal
Oct 8	Determine Theme	Document Evidence to Support Theme	
Oct 15	Determine Theme	Document Evidence to Support Theme	
Oct 22	Determine Theme	Document Evidence to Support Theme	
Oct 29	Determine Theme	Document Evidence to Support Theme	Nov 1
Nov 5	Use evidence to support my opinion in an essay	Learn how to write a literary essay	
Nov. 12	Use evidence to support my opinion in an essay	Learn how to write a literary essay	

Voices from the Classroom

Triangulating Data with Students

Clare met with Jonah to talk about the goals he set to increase the amount he was reading and looked at the display, or book log, he was using to assess his progress.

"So, Jonah, how's it going with reading?"

"Fine."

"Let's take a look at your log and see how you are progressing on your goal of reading for more time each day and night."

Clare noticed Jonah squirm a bit and look at the clock as she turned to his reading log. "What has he done?" she thought to herself. "Today is Tuesday, but he has filled in his log through next Sunday." She took a breath.

"So, Jonah, tell me about how you have been using your log to increase your reading time at home."

Silence. Clare waited him out.

"Well, my reading time is really getting better. I am reading for longer."

"That is great! Can you show how you are using your log to track that?"

"Well, that's the thing. I don't really understand how this log is supposed to help me read longer, but I know I'm supposed to do it. So I planned on how much I should read each day and night to finish the book by Sunday, and I wrote that in the log. I know it's not a log, but I don't see how writing how long I read after I read will help me read longer."

Clare had gone from thinking he was faking his reading to thinking he was brilliant. Her pause had caused him to panic.

"I'm sorry I did it wrong. I'll fix it."

"No, Jonah. What you did was so smart! You created a display that will help you plan your reading so you can meet your goals. That makes perfect sense. How do you know if you met your goal?"

"There is not a column for that."

"How would you structure the display to show that?"

Jonah immediately began to create a display that would help him, and Clare realized that seeing the purpose in the displays would help her students use them. ◄

Assessment and the Growth Mind-Set

As teachers we typically only get the privilege of knowing our readers for one year or one chapter of their story. Each reader, therefore, needs to be aware of her story and carry it with her throughout her school journey. When our readers have a growth mind-set (Dweck 2006), they believe that their basic qualities are things they can cultivate through their efforts. Everyone can change and grow with instruction, feedback, practice, and reflection. "The passion for stretching yourself and sticking to it, even (or especially) when it is not going well, is the hallmark of the growth mindset. It is this mindset that allows people to thrive during some of the most challenging times in their lives" (Dweck 2006, 7). Our readers need to know and believe that they have the power to set and meet their goals and that school is a place where it can happen. It is our responsibility to make school this place. School needs to be about more than standards, levels, and proficiencies. School needs to be a place where one grows and learns how to be a learner.

Our readers need to know that no one has the right to define them as a number and that they are the most important force behind their own growth. As Peter Johnston reminds us, "If nothing else, children should leave school with a sense that if they act, and act strategically, they can accomplish their goals. I call this feeling a sense of agency" (2004, 29). This sense of agency will give them the confidence to speak honestly about their process of learning and to view assessment as a tool for their continued growth and learning as a reader. When we cultivate a growth mind-set—a belief that growth is about motivation, hard work, instruction, and practice—our students will know that they have the power to change and achieve their goals. When we empower our readers to engage in assessing and learning, we truly give them the gift of lifelong learning and joy in the pursuit of understanding.

THE STORIES WE CARRY

Assessment and the Growth Mind-Set

Timmy was a second grader. He struggled throughout first grade and never really began strategically reading. He started second grade frustrated with learning. No matter what we did, he had a reason he was not going to do it. He had given up and was not engaged in any of our instruction.

We decided to have a conversation with Timmy. We shared his conference notes with him and discussed our concerns. We asked him to share his thoughts and concerns. No eye contact, no response. We waited a bit, but it was clear he did not want to engage in the conversation. "We need your help, Timmy. We know it's frustrating, but we also know you are going to learn how to read. We cannot teach you unless you help us understand what is going on for you as a reader. Let's plan on talking again tomorrow."

About an hour later, Timmy came up to us and handed us the drawing in Figure S6.1. Now, there was a lot for us to assess in terms of his literacy in this drawing, but what was most striking to us was that Timmy was now in the game. By giving us this drawing, he was taking a risk and believing he could learn. He had taken the first step. We looked up to see him crying and still avoiding eye contact.

Figure S6.1
Timmy's
Note to Us

"Okay. This is really helpful. We can see from your drawing that you are really frustrated and your words help us know why you are frustrated. This is exactly what we need to teach you how to read. We can totally show you how to do it, but we need to know that you want to learn how to do it. Do you want to learn how to do it?"

He nodded his head, tears still streaming down his face.

"Okay. Now, this is not going to be easy, and it's going to take some time. You are going to have to work hard and let us know how it's going for you. We are going to set goals and keep track of those goals. Is that okay with you?"

"Will I learn to read?" he asked.

"Yes—if you work hard and talk to us about how your learning is going, you will learn how to read."

Six months later our class was studying folktales and Timmy wrote this one:

The Snake Who Doesn't Know How to Read

A long time ago, a snake did not know how to read. The snake went to the teachers and told them he did not know how to read. He asked them, "How do I do it?" She is going to teach him how to sound out the words. Then he learns it later on. Then he asked the teacher, "How do you break words up?" The teacher said, "Look for little words." Then Snake tried it. Then later on snake learned how to read. Snake felt good. The lesson is: Keep trying to read.

Epilogue

We ended this book with Timmy's story because although we carry all these stories with us every day to remember what is important to us in teaching and learning, the message in his story is one we hope we never forget. We need to keep trying and growing. We need to remember this lesson professionally in our work with our readers. No matter what we are teaching, we need to embed the lesson—keep trying—into the content. This message is really about assessment. Assessment is the tool we use to understand the story of our readers so that we know how to teach them and give them the motivation to keep trying. If we use assessment to understand, not evaluate, then it becomes the key to growth. It is how we use and talk about assessment that makes the difference in the mind-set of our readers and gives us the motivation to keep trying to be the best teachers we can be.

Appendix

CONFERRING NOTES

Student Name:

Goals:
-
-
-

Date/Title	Observation and Instruction Notes	Instructional Goals: Next Steps to Meet Goals

Engagement   Text   Metacognition   Reader Response

SMALL-GROUP INSTRUCTION FOR GUIDED PRACTICE

Names of Students	Instructional Goals	Frequency of Group
Names of Students	Instructional Goals	Frequency of Group
Names of Students	Instructional Goals	Frequency of Group
Names of Students	Instructional Goals	Frequency of Group

Conferences			
Name(s)	Instructional Goal	Name(s)	Instructional Goal

Engagement   **Text**   **Metacognition**   **Reader Response**

LESSON PLANNING FORM

Anchor Lesson:		
Pre-assessment		**Notes to Build Next Lesson**
Select the materials.		
Name the strategy. Explain. *"I have noticed that . . ."* *"A strategy readers use is . . ."*		
Demonstrate the strategy. **Say:** *Think aloud.* **Show:** *Model.* **Explain:** *How this will help them as a reader.*		
Provide guided practice. Invite the students to practice the strategy with teacher guidance.		
Provide independent practice. Remind students before they go off to reading workshop.		
Conference Points		
Share/Reinforce		

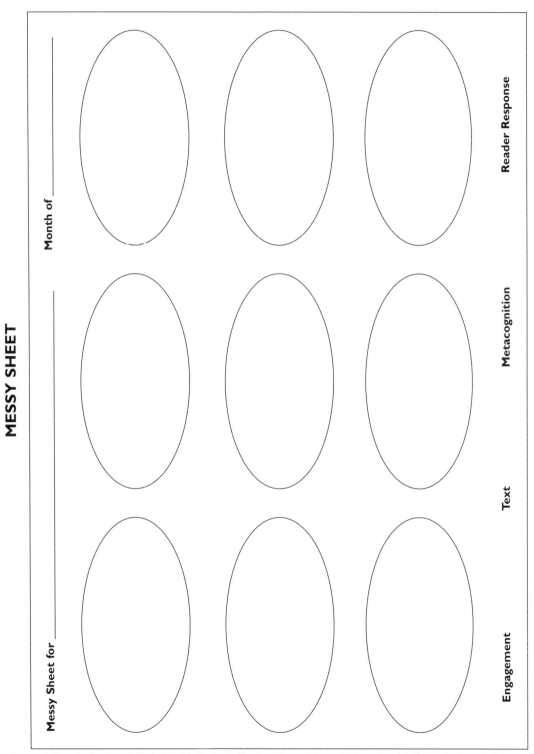

MESSY SHEET

Month of _____

Messy Sheet for _____

Reader Response

Metacognition

Text

Engagement

Bibliography

Allen, Jennifer. 2006. *Becoming a Literacy Leader: Supporting Learning and Change*. Portland, ME: Stenhouse.

Allison, Dorothy. 1995. *Two or Three Things I Know for Sure*. New York: Penguin.

Black, Paul, and Dylan William. 1998. "Inside the Black Box: Raising Standards Through Classroom Assessment." *Phi Delta Kappan*. www.pdkintl.org/kappan/kbla9810.htm.

Boudett, Kathryn Parker, Elizabeth A. City, and Richard J. Murnane. 2005. *Data Wise: A Step–by–Step Guide to Using Assessment Results to Improve Teaching and Learning*. Cambridge, MA: Harvard Education Press.

Boushey, Gail, and Joan Moser. 2009. *The CAFE Book: Engaging All Students in Daily Literacy Assessment and Instruction*. Portland, ME: Stenhouse.

Brookhart, Susan M. 2008. *How to Give Effective Feedback to Your Students*. Alexandria, VA: ASCD.

———. 2009. *Advancing Formative Assessment in Every Classroom: A Guide for Instructional Leaders*. Alexandria, VA: ASCD.

Buckner, Aimee. 2009. *Notebook Connections: Strategies for the Reader's Notebook*. Portland, ME: Stenhouse.

Calkins, Lucy. 2001. *The Art of Teaching Reading*. Boston: Allyn and Bacon.

———. 2003. *The Nuts and Bolts of Teaching Writing*. Portsmouth, NH: Heinemann.

Calkins, Lucy, Mary Ehrenworth, and Christopher Lehman. 2012. *Pathways to the Common Core.* Portsmouth, NH: Heinemann.

Clay, Marie. 1993. *An Observation Survey.* Portsmouth, NH: Heinemann.

Coles, Robert. 1989. *The Call of Stories. Teaching and the Moral Imagination.* Boston: Houghton Mifflin.

Collins, Kathy. 2004. *Growing Readers.* Portland, ME: Stenhouse.

Common Core State Standards Initiative. 2012. "Frequently Asked Questions." www.corestandards.org/resources/frequently-asked-questions.

Dweck, Carol. 2006. *Mindset: The New Psychology of Success.* New York: Random House.

Elkind, David. 1969. "Piagetian and Psychometric Conceptions of Intelligence." *Harvard Educational Review* 39:319–337.

Fullan, Michael. 2011. *The Six Secrets of Change: What the Best Leaders Do to Help Their Organizations Survive and Thrive.* San Francisco: Jossey–Bass.

Gulati, Basia Miller. 1977. *Conversations with Jean Piaget.* Chicago: University of Chicago Press.

Johnston, Peter. 1997. *Knowing Literacy: Constructing Literacy Assessment.* Portland, ME: Stenhouse.

———. 2004. *Choice Words: How Our Language Affects Children's Learning.* Portland, ME: Stenhouse.

———. 2012. *Opening Minds: Using Language to Change Lives.* Portland, ME: Stenhouse.

Logsdon, Ann. 2012. "Norm-Referenced Tests—What Are Norm-Referenced Tests?" http://learningdisabilities.about.com/od/mo/g/normreferenced.htm.

Marzano, Robert J., and Mark W. Haystead. 2008. *Making Standards Useful in the Classroom.* Alexandria, VA: ASCD.

McLeod, S. A. 2009. *Jean Piaget: Cognitive Development.* www.simplypsychology.org/piaget.html.

Miller, Debbie. 2008. *Teaching with Intention: Defining Beliefs, Aligning Practice, Taking Action.* Portland, ME: Stenhouse.

National Center on Response to Intervention. 2010. "Essential Components of RTI—A Closer Look at Response to Intervention." Washington, DC: U.S. Department of Education, Office of Special Education Programs, National Center on Response to Intervention.

National Governors Association (NGA) Center for Best Practices and Council of Chief State School Officers (CCSSO). 2010. "Common Core State Standards." Washington, DC: National Governors Association Center for Best Practices, Council of Chief State School Officers.

National Reading Panel. 2000. "Frequently Asked Questions." www.nationalreadingpanel.org/FAQ/faq.htm.

Paley, V. G. 1997. Introduction to *Class Acts: Teachers Reflect on Their Own Classroom Practice*, ed. I. Hall, C. H. Campbell, and E. J. Miech. Cambridge, MA: Harvard University Press.

Pearson, P. David, and M. C. Gallagher. 1983. "The Instruction of Reading Comprehension." *Contemporary Educational Psychology* 8:317–344.

Pink, Daniel. 2011. *Drive: The Surprising Truth About What Motivates Us*. New York: Penguin.

Pollock, E. Jane. 2012. *Feedback: The Hinge That Joins Teaching and Learning*. Thousand Oaks, CA: Corwin Sage.

Popham, W. James. 2004. "Why Assessment Illiteracy Is Professional Suicide" E*ducational Leadership* 62:82–83.

———. 2009. "Is Assessment Literacy the Magic Bullet?" *Voices in Education*. Harvard Education Publishing Group. www.hepg.org/blog/19.

Rapp, Katie. 2012. "Quality Feedback: What Is It and How to Give It." *Educational Update*. http://www.ascd.org/ascd-express/vol8/801-rapp.aspx.

Reading Rockets. 2013. www.readingrockets.org.

Routman, Regie. 2005. *Writing Essentials: Raising Expectations and Results While Simplifying Teaching*. Portsmouth, NH: Heinemann.

Schmoker, Mike. 2008/2009. "Measuring What Matters." *Educational Leadership* 66:70–74.

———. 2011. "Curriculum Now." *Phi Delta Kappan* 93:70–71.

Serravallo, Jennifer. 2010. *Teaching Reading in Small Groups: Differentiated Instruction for Building Strategic, Independent Readers*. Portsmouth, NH: Heinemann.

Sibberson, Franki, and Karen Szymusiak. 2003. *Still Learning to Read: Teaching Students in Grades 3–6*. Portland, ME: Stenhouse.

Stake, Robert, cited in Lorna Earl. 2004. *Assessment as Learning: Using Classroom Achievement to Maximize Student Learning*. Thousand Oaks, CA: Corwin.

Stiggins, Rick, and Chappuis, Jan. 2008. "Enhancing Student Learning." *District Administration Magazine.* http://ati.pearson.com/downloads/enhancingstudent_dadmn01–08.pdf.

Strahan, David, and Carrie Rogers. 2012. *Research Summary: Formative Assessment Practices in Successful Middle Level Classrooms.* www.amle.org/portals/0/pdf/research/Research_Summaries/Formative_Assessment.pdf.

Teachers College Reading and Writing Project. 2010. http://readingandwritingproject.com/resources/assessments/performance–assessments.html.

Tomlinson, Carol A. 1999. *The Differentiated Classroom: Responding to the Needs of All Learners.* Alexandria, VA: ASCD.

Tomlinson, Carol A., and Jay McTighe. 2006. *Integrating Differentiated Instruction & Understanding by Design: Connecting Content and Kids.* Alexandria, VA: ASCD.

Tovani, Cris. 2011. *So What Do They Really Know? Assessment That Informs Teaching and Learning.* Portland, ME: Stenhouse.

Vygotsky, L. S. 1978. *Mind in Society: The Development of Higher Psychological Processes.* Cambridge, MA: Harvard University Press.

Wiggins, Grant. 1998. *Educative Assessment: Designing Assessments to Inform and Improve Student Performance.* San Francisco: Jossey–Bass.

———. 2012. "Seven Keys to Effective Feedback." *Educational Leadership* 70:10–16.

Index

Page numbers followed by an *f* indicate figures.

A

accountability, 13–14

accuracy, 34–38, 34*f*, 36*f*–37*f*

Advancing Formative Assessment in Every Classroom: A Guide for Instructional Leaders (Brookhart), 108

AIMSweb, 31*f*, 37*f*

Allen, Jennifer, 67

analyzing. *See also* triangulating data
    instruction and, 72–74
    recording observations and, 77–81, 78*f*, 79, 80*f*

Angelou, Maya, 42

assessing. *See also* triangulating data
    instruction and, 72–74
    recording observations and, 77–81, 78*f*, 79, 80*f*

Assessment as Learning (Stake), 20

assessment literacy
    areas of reading measured by assessments, 34–38, 34*f*, 36f–37*f*
    building, 32–33
    example of, 40–42, 113
    overview, 20–22, 21*f*, 105–112, 110*f*

assessment overview, 2–4
    areas of reading measured by assessments, 34–38, 34*f*, 36f–37*f*
    categories of assessments, 21–22, 21*f*, 28–32, 30f–31*f*, 48

data type, 25, 26–28, 28*f*

design of assessment, 21–22, 21*f*

instruction and, 9–15, 10*f*, 13*f*

method for assessing, 21*f*, 24–25, 26*f*

purpose of assessment, 21*f*, 22–23

B

bar graphs, 52–53, 53*f*

Becoming a Literacy Leader (Allen), 67

Benchmark Assessment System, 30*f*, 35, 36*f*, 96*f*

benchmarks, 65

book logs, 74, 88, 109–111, 110*f*

Boushey, Gail, 85

Brookhart, Susan M., 101, 108

Buckner, Aimee, 86–87

C

CAFE Menu, 62, 63*f*, 65

Calkins, Lucy, 2–3, 39*f*, 75

Cambourne, Brian, 8

categories of assessments, 21–22, 21*f*, 28–32, 30f–31*f*, 36f–37*f*, 48

classroom assessments
    example of, 74–81, 94–98, 94*f*, 95*f*, 96f, 97*f*, 98*f*
    using displays to highlight patterns in, 90–93, 91*f*, 92*f*, 93*f*

classroom data, 74. *See also* classroom assessments; instruction

Clay, Marie, 9, 46, 73–74, 78

Collins, Kathy, 75

common assessments, 30*f*–31*f*, 36*f*–37*f*, 38, 39*f*, 40–42, 50–51

Common Core State Standards, 14–15, 39*f*. *See also* standards

comprehension, 34–38, 34*f*, 36*f*–37*f*

concepts about print, 34–38, 34*f*, 36*f*–37*f*

conference framework, 75

conference notes. *See also* observations

  example of, 77–90, 95*f*, 97*f*, 104–105

  form for, 126

  housing notes, 82–84, 82*f*, 83*f*

  overview, 74, 77–78

  Reading Conference Notes, 36*f*

  sharing notes, 86

  taking effective notes, 84–86, 85*f*

  using to triangulate data, 59–60, 59*f*

constructed responses, 74, 88–89, 112. *See also* student work in assessment

CORE Literacy Library, 30*f*–31*f*, 35, 37*f*

curriculum-based measurements (CBM), 38

D

data. *See* assessment overview

  example of, 16–17

  overview, 5–6

  sharing with students, 100–105

data type

  assessment literacy and, 107–112, 110*f*

  overview, 25, 26–28, 28*f*

data walls, 55–58, 55*f*, 56*f*, 65

design of assessment, 21–22, 21*f*, 30*f*–31*f*, 64–65

developmentally appropriate instruction, 11–15, 13*f*. *See also* instruction

Developmental Reading Assessment, Second Edition (DRA2)

  areas of reading measured by, 30*f*, 35, 36*f*

  assessment literacy and, 109

  example of, 49–50, 69–70

  overview, 35

developmental theory of learning, 11–12

diagnostic assessment

  assessment literacy and, 109, 112

  design of assessment, 21–23, 21*f*

  overlap with other assessment categories and, 28–32, 30*f*–31*f*

  purpose of assessment, 22–23

self-reflection and, 31–32

state test and, 32

student-constructed responses and, 88–89

triangulating data and, 49*f*, 51

using displays to highlight patterns in, 90–93, 91*f*, 92*f*, 93*f*

differentiated instruction, 9–10. *See also* instruction

displays

  example of, 66–70, 68*f*, 94–98, 94*f*, 95*f*, 96*f*, 97*f*, 98*f*

  jump-starting the assessment process and, 64–65

  power of, 51–52

  using to highlight patterns in assessment data, 90–93, 91*f*, 92*f*, 93*f*

  using to triangulate data, 52–64, 53*f*, 54*f*, 55*f*, 56*f*, 58*f*, 59*f*, 60*f*, 61*f*, 62*f*, 63*f*, 68–70, 68*f*

Dweck, 101

Dynamic Indicator of Basic Early Literacy Skills (DIBELS) assessment, 31*f*, 35, 37*f*, 41–42

dynamic-learning framework, 101–103, 102*f*

E

engagement notes, 74, 81. *See also* observations

F

feedback

  assessment literacy and, 105–112

  example of, 104–105

  overview, 103

Feedback: The Hinge That Joins Teaching and Learning (Pollock), 114

fixed-performance framework, 101–103, 102*f*, 113–114

fluency, 34–38, 34*f*, 36*f*–37*f*

formal assessment

  assessment literacy and, 107

  design of assessment, 21–22, 21*f*

  method for assessing, 24–25

  overlap with other assessment categories and, 28–32, 30*f*–31f

  overview, 24–25

  triangulating data and, 49*f*, 50–51

formative assessment

  assessment literacy and, 111–112

  design of assessment, 21–22, 21*f*

feedback and, 103

overlap with other assessment categories and, 28–32, 30*f*–31*f*

overview, 23

purpose of assessment, 22–23

recording observations and, 77–81, 78*f*, 79*f*, 80*f*

self-reflection and, 31–32

triangulating data and, 49*f*

using displays to highlight patterns in, 90–93, 91*f*, 92*f*, 93*f*

Fountas and Pinnell Benchmark Assessment System, 30*f*, 35, 36*f*

G

Gallagher, Margaret C., 10, 73

goals of instruction. *See also* instruction

assessment literacy and, 105–112, 110*f*

discussing with readers, 104–105

example of, 94–98, 94*f*, 95*f*, 96*f*, 97*f*, 98*f*, 104–105

lesson structure and, 77

small-group notes and, 79, 80*f*

triangulating data with students and, 113–118, 115*f*, 116*f*, 117*f*

grade equivalent (GE), 26*f*

gradual release of responsibility model of instruction, 10, 10*f*, 73, 75

Group Reading Assessment and Diagnostic Evaluation (GRADE)

areas of reading measured by, 30*f*, 35, 36*f*

assessment literacy and, 20

triangulating data and, 51

Growing Readers (Collins), 75

growth mind-set theory, 101–103, 102*f*, 118–119, 120–121

H

Haystead, Mark, 101

high-frequency words, 30*f*, 34–38, 34*f*, 36*f*, 36*f*–37*f*

How to Give Effective Feedback to Your Students (Brookhart), 101

I

individual lessons, 75, 79. *See also* instruction

informal assessment

assessment literacy and, 107

definition of, 24

design of assessment, 21–22, 21*f*

method for assessing, 24

overlap with other assessment categories and, 28–32, 30*f*–31*f*

recording observations and, 77–81, 78*f*, 79*f*, 80*f*

triangulating data and, 49*f*, 50–51

informal tests, 74. *See also* student work in assessment

initial sound fluency, 35

instruction. *See also* instructional goals

assessment and, 9–10, 10*f*, 35

developmentally appropriateness of, 11–15, 13*f*

example of, 94–98, 94*f*, 95*f*, 96*f*, 97*f*, 98*f*

feedback and, 103

overview, 72–74, 101–104, 102*f*

standards and, 11–15, 13*f*

structures and, 75–77, 76*f*

triangulating data with students and, 113–118, 115*f*, 116*f*, 117*f*

using displays to highlight patterns in assessment data and, 90–93, 91*f*, 92*f*, 93f

instructional goals. *See also* instruction

assessment literacy and, 105–112

discussing with readers, 104–105

example of, 94–98, 94*f*, 95*f*, 96*f*, 97*f*, 98*f*, 104–105

lesson structure and, 75–77, 76*f*

small-group notes and, 79, 80*f*

triangulating data with students and, 113–118, 115*f*, 116*f*, 117*f*

inventories, 74. *See also* observations

J

Johnston, Peter, 9, 73, 100, 101–103, 102*f*, 119

jump-starting the assessment process, 64–65

L

learning experiences, 13

lesson planning, 81, 128

lesson structure, 75–77, 76*f*. *See also* instruction; structures

letter naming fluency, 66

Lexia Quick Reading Test, 31*f*, 37*f*, 50

line graphs

example of, 68–69, 68*f*

using to triangulate data, 58–59, 58*f*

literacy literacy, 34–38, 34*f*, 36*f*–37*f*
logs, 74, 88, 109–111, 110*f. See also* student work in assessment

M

Making Standards Useful in the Classroom (Marzano and Haystead), 101
Marzano, Robert, 101
Messy Sheet
    form for, 129
    jump-starting the assessment process and, 65
    turn-and-talk notes and, 81
    using to highlight patterns in assessment data, 90–93, 91*f*, 92*f*, 93*f*
    using to triangulate data, 60–61, 61*f*
method for assessing, 24–25, 107
Miller, Debbie, 8–9, 14–15
Moser, Joan, 85

N

Names Assessment, 31*f*, 37*f*
needs of students, 94–98, 94*f*, 95*f*, 96*f*, 97*f*, 98*f*
No Child Left Behind Act, 3
nonsense word fluency, 35, 67
norm-referenced assessment, 26*f*
Northwest Evaluation Association (NWEA), 30*f*, 36*f*
Notebook Connections (Buckner), 86–87
notebook entries. *See also* student work in assessment
    assessment literacy and, 111–112
    recording data from, 86–89, 87*f*, 88*f*
note taking
    example of, 94–98
    housing notes, 82–84, 82*f*, 83*f*
    recording observations and, 77–81, 78*f*, 79*f*, 80*f*
    sharing notes, 86
    student work and, 86–89, 87*f*, 88*f*
    taking effective notes, 84–86, 85*f*

O

observations. *See also* running record
    example of, 89–90
    housing notes, 82–84, 82*f*, 83*f*
    Observation Survey, 30*f*, 36*f*
    recording, 77–81, 78*f*, 79*f*, 80*f*
    sharing notes, 86

    structures and, 75–77, 76*f*
    taking effective notes, 84–86, 85*f*
Observation Survey, The (Clay), 78
ongoing assessments, 77–81, 78*f*, 79*f*, 80*f*
open/constructed responses, 74, 88–89, 112
Opening Minds (Johnston), 100

P

Partnership for Assessment of Readiness for College and Careers (PARCC), 39*f*
Pathways to the Common Core (Calkins), 39*f*
Pearson, P. David, 10, 73
percentile rank, 26*f*
performance assessments, 40
performance level, 26*f*
phoneme segmentation, 35, 66–67
phonemic awareness, 34–38, 34*f*, 36*f*–37*f*, 66–67
phonics, 30*f*–31*f*, 34–38, 34*f*, 36*f*–37*f*
Phonological Awareness Skills Text (PAST), 31*f*, 37*f*
Piaget, Jean, 11, 12, 73
picture graphs
    jump-starting the assessment process and, 65
    using to triangulate data (overview), 61–62, 62*f*
Pink, Daniel, 93
Pollock, Jane E., 114
progress monitoring, 40
projects, 74. *See also* student work in assessment
purpose of assessment, 22–23, 49*f*, 106

Q

qualitative assessment
    assessment literacy and, 107–112, 110*f*
    data type, 25, 26–28, 28*f*
    design of assessment, 21–22, 21*f*
    overlap with other assessment categories and, 28–32, 30*f*–31*f*
    triangulating data and, 49*f*
Qualitative Reading Inventory, Fourth Edition (QRI-4), 36*f*
quantitative assessment
    data type, 25, 26–28, 28*f*
    design of assessment, 21–22, 21*f*
    overlap with other assessment categories and, 28–32, 30*f*–31*f*
    triangulating data and, 49*f*
questioning. *See* triangulating data

instruction and, 72–74
    recording observations and, 77–81, 78*f*, 79*f*, 80*f*
Quick Phonics Screener, 37*f*

R

Rapp, Katie, 105
raw score, 26*f*
reading (areas to measure), 34–38, 34*f*, 36*f*–37*f*
reading behavior notes, 74, 78–79, 78*f*, 79*f*. *See
    also* observations
reading disposition, 34–38, 34*f*, 36*f*–37*f*
recording observations, 77–81, 78*f*, 79*f*, 80*f*
reflections, 74, 86–89, 87*f*, 88*f*. *See also* student
    work in assessment
Response to Intervention (RTI) legislation,
    38–40, 39*f*, 86
retelling, 109
running record. *See also* observations
    areas of reading measured by, 36*f*
    assessment literacy and, 33, 108–109
    categories of assessments and, 29, 30*f*–31f
    example of, 28*f*
    overview, 27–28, 74, 78–79
    using to triangulate data, 62–64, 63*f*

S

screener, 41–42
self-reflection, 31–32, 36*f*
Serravallo, Jennifer, 81
Sibberson, Franki, 111
small-group notes. *See also* observations
    example of, 89–90
    form for, 127
    housing notes, 83–84
    overview, 74, 79, 80*f*
small-group work, 75, 79. *See also* instruction;
    small-group notes
Smarter Balanced Assessment Consortium
    (SBAC), 39*f*
social-constructive theory, 101–103, 102*f*
So What Do They Really Know? (Tovani), 72
Stake, Robert, 20
standards, 11–15, 13*f*, 26*f*
Stanford Achievement Text Series, Tenth Edition
    (Stanford 10), 36*f*
stanine, 26*f*
state test, 30f

areas of reading measured by, 36*f*
    assessment literacy, 32–33
    categories of assessments, 32
    triangulating data and, 51
stem-and-leaf graphs, 53–55, 54*f*, 65, 66
strategy inventory. *See also* observations
    example of, 98*f*
    overview, 78–79, 78*f*
    triangulating data with students and, 116, 116*f*
structures, 75–77, 76*f*
students. *See also* student work in assessment
    assessment literacy and, 105–112, 110*f*
    growth mind-set theory and, 118–119
    role of in assessment, 103
    triangulating data with, 113–118, 115*f*, 116*f*,
        117*f*
student work in assessment
    areas of reading measured by, 36*f*
    overview, 74
    recording data from, 86–89, 87*f*, 88*f*
summative assessment
    design of assessment, 21–22, 21*f*
    overlap with other assessment categories and,
        28–32, 30*f*–31*f*
    purpose of assessment, 22–23
    self-reflection and, 31–32
    state test and, 32
    triangulating data and, 49*f*
    using displays to highlight patterns in, 90–93,
        91*f*, 92*f*, 93*f*
surveys, 74. *See also* student work in assessment
Szymusiak, Karen, 111

T

Teachers College Common-Core-Aligned
    Performance Assessments, 30*f*, 36*f*
Teachers College Fiction Reading Assessments,
    30*f*, 36*f*
teaching, 72–74. *See also* instruction
Teaching Reading in Small Groups (Serravallo), 81
TerraNova, 30*f*, 36*f*
time samplings, 74. *See also* observations
Tomlinson, Carol Ann, 10, 73
Tovani, Cris, 72
triangulating data
    displays and, 51–64, 53*f*, 54*f*, 55*f*, 56*f*, 58*f*, 59*f*,
        60*f*, 61*f*, 62*f*, 63*f*

triangulating data *(continued)*
  example of, 66–70, 68*f*, 89–90, 94–98, 94*f*, 95*f*,
    96*f*, 97*f*, 98*f*, 117–118
  instruction and, 72–74
  involving readers in, 113–118, 115*f*, 116*f*, 117*f*
  jump-starting the assessment process, 64–65
  overview, 47–51, 49*f*, 51*f*
  recording observations and, 77–81, 78*f*, 79*f*, 80*f*
  using displays to highlight patterns in
    assessment data and, 90–93, 91*f*, 92*f*, 93*f*
turn-and-talk notes, 74, 81. *See also* observations
Two or Three Things I Know for Sure (Allison), 8

U
universal screeners, 40

V
vocabulary, 34–38, 34*f*, 36f–37*f*
Vygotsky, Lev, 11, 73

W
whole-class instruction, 75, 79. *See also*
    instruction
Williams, William Carlos, 2
Words Their Way Spelling Inventories, 31*f*, 37*f*
workshop model, 75–77, 76*f*

Z
zone of proximal development, 11